GREAT RUGBY PLAYERS

GREAT RUGBY PLAYERS

David Norrie

HAMLYN

LONDON·NEW YORK·SYDNEY·TORONTO

To my father
for showing such enthusiasm
. . . and tolerance!

Acknowledgements

Colour Agence Presse Sports, Paris 30, 34, 46–47, 66–67, 71 top, 78, 86, 103, 106, 107, 119, 126, 131, 138, 142–143, 151, 158; All-Sport, Morden 50, 55 top, 94; All-Sport – Adrian Murrell 2–3; Colorsport, London 10, 22, 38, 42, 58–59, 111, 135, 170, 171.

Black and white Agence Presse Sports, Paris 62, 68, 93, 120, 123, 139, 144, 152, 155, 161, 172–173; All-Sport, Morden – Adrian Murrell 27, 136; Associated Press, London 20–21, 82, 156; Auckland Star 128; Mike Brett Photography, Sale endpapers, 11; Central Press Photos, London 13, 81, 113, 122; Colorsport, London 1, 6–7, 28, 35, 39 top, 39 bottom, 40, 41, 45, 49 top, 49 bottom, 55 bottom, 57, 60, 71 bottom, 97, 100, 104–105, 141; Colin Elsey, London 37, 44, 79, 91, 108; Evening Post, Wellington 24, 110, 164; George P. Herringshaw, Leicester 77, 133; Keystone Press Agency, London 32; E. D. Lacey, Leatherhead 9; New Zealand Herald, Auckland 63, 85, 147; New Zealand Information Service 59 top; *Rugby World*, Sutton 117, 121, 167; Scotsman Publications, Edinburgh 72; Sport and General Press Agency, London 17, 31, 53, 65, 74, 75, 88, 90, 116, 149, 150, 160, 162–163; Sporting Pictures (UK), London 169; D. R. Stuart, London 89; Bob Thomas, Northampton 125; Topix, London 19.

We would like to thank *Rugby World* for their help in supplying photographs

Published 1980 by
The Hamlyn Publishing Group Limited
London · New York · Sydney · Toronto
Astronaut House, Feltham, Middlesex, England

© Copyright 1980 The Hamlyn Publishing Group Limited

ISBN 0 600 37191 3

Filmset by Tradespools Limited, Frome, Somerset
Printed and bound in Spain

Contents

Introduction

The Great Rugby Players. Fifty of them, since the War. Not the greatest fifty; just fifty who have contributed a vast amount to the game of Rugby football over the past thirty-five years. Time, circumstance, nationality and the very nature of Rugby would make a definitive selection impossible and ridiculous. I realise that many future conversations will begin, and end, with: 'How on earth could you leave . . . out?' A question for which, of course, there is no convincing answer. The great Rugby players are not limited to those who find themselves in this book.

Yet, all the players here have been tremendous servants of their countries and of the game in general. They will linger long in the memory as their magical moments on the Rugby field already do. All, without exception, have enhanced the great game of Rugby Union. And it is a game that throws up a variety of skills – the grace of Butterfield and Gibson, the power of Meads, the hypnotising running of Jackson, the competitiveness of JPR, the dedication of McBride and McLauchlan, the strength of Gray . . . the list is endless and it is this variety of skill and character that will ensure the survival of the game we love.

David Norrie
1980

Opposite: *Willie John McBride, obviously relishing the physical battle, bursts through Andy Ripley's tackle in the game against England at Twickenham in 1972.*

Great Rugby Players

Phil Bennett

Phil Bennett was the wizard at fly-half who followed Barry John into the Welsh side and then followed him into the ranks of Wales' Rugby heroes. A diminutive, frail-looking, dark-haired player he seemed to be continually wearing red. Did he ever change his jersey, or was it just an unceasing swapping of the badges of Llanelli, Wales and the British Lions? 'Benny' served them all with great distinction. For a man who looked as though a strong gust of wind would blow him over, he had amazing resilience and courage; he totally belied his size as he dominated matches at the highest level.

After taking the role of Wales' utility back in the early days of his international career and waiting for Barry John to retire, Bennett emerged in many ways as a greater match-winner than his illustrious predecessor, although not in John's class as a linkman or feeder of his backs. Bennett's kicking out of hand, whether up the touchline or tactically, was of such precision that many wondered if he had a remote control, so well did the ball obey the instructions of his kicking boot. His place-kicking was in the same class; one hundred and sixty-six international points for Wales and another forty-four in Lions' Tests. If he had satisfied himself with his kicking skills alone, Bennett would still have been an international. Yet he had the ability to launch attacks from everywhere, usually leaving defences in states of chaos. His three sidesteps in the 1973 Barbarians-All Blacks' classic were contemptuous of all danger and inspired from above, and when Gareth Edwards dived over all those heart-beating

seconds later, it was rightly credited as one of the finest team-tries ever.

Throughout Bennett's career, confidence was the key to this complex, sensitive, retiring Welshman, who is never happier than when in his native Llanelli. On the 1974 Lions' tour, he formed a close friendship with Willie John McBride, his captain, who provided strong support for the Welshman for whom homesickness was a serious problem. But, in 1977 there was no McBride and, in addition, Bennett was the captain; apart from one or two odd flashes, the fly-half did not do himself justice, nagging injuries not helping. Not that he was an unpopular captain; his team-mates were ready to defend the 'wee man' to the ends of the earth. It was just that the position of captain was a responsibility he could have done without. Perhaps he was too emotional for the post; defeat would show on his face and there was a sadness in his eyes that mirrored real suffering. But, even with his problems in attack in New Zealand, especially when he started shuffling across the field, cramping his backs, there was one aspect of his game that had never been better. His covering tackles in defence, very reminiscent of Cliff Morgan, were superb. He often saved the situation with a last-ditch tackle, not only for the Lions but many times for Wales and Llanelli; his courage was undeniable.

Bennett was one of the major reasons for the success of British Rugby in the seventies, fulfilling a promise that had been spotted long before he ever made the Llanelli first

A familiar sight in the seventies – Phil Bennett slotting the ball over at the Arms Park for Wales.

8

team. He was a schools and youth international, being particularly outstanding in 1967 in his final youth game, against France at Stradey Park – the Rugby ground he was to grace many times in the future. Even though Barry John was at Llanelli, Bennett joined the club, and was able to establish himself in the fly-half berth when John left to play for Cardiff. His early international career was rather haphazard; without playing in the Tests, there were visits to Argentina (1968) and New Zealand (1969). Bennett was already capped when the All Blacks were faced; in the 1968-69

season he had become Wales' first-ever replacement when Gerald Davies went off with three minutes to go in the game against France and Bennett made his debut without even touching the ball. The next season, he was to be found on the right wing against the Springboks, in the centre against Scotland, dropped for the following two games and eventually he replaced the injured Barry John before the final game against France. Bennett was not to be found at all on the international field in 1971, also narrowly missing selection for the Lions, and his only other cap before Barry

Not in a red jersey for once, Phil Bennett jumps out of a Penarth tackle while playing for the Barbarians on their Easter tour in 1978.

Opposite: *The Lions' fly-half and captain, Phil Bennett, on the attack in the 1977 game against Auckland.*

Phil Bennett, clutching the ball, looks down the pitch after scoring the try of the season against Scotland at Murrayfield in 1977.

John retired in 1972 was the game against Scotland, as a replacement again, when JPR Williams had his jaw broken by Billy Steele's tackle.

For Bennett, the 1972-73 season was the realisation of many dreams – Llanelli beat the All Blacks and won the WRU Cup; he was established as the Welsh fly-half in their five internationals; and more than played his part in the Baa-Baas' thrilling 23-11 win over Kirkpatrick's side. But life only got better the following year – he played throughout for Wales and then travelled to South Africa to astound the Springboks with some of the most exciting displays ever produced by a fly-half. It was that Barbarians' magic all over again; he ran, jinked, sidestepped, dummied as he had never done before and the Lions ran

the Springboks ragged with five tries in the second Test and three in the third. It did not matter whether Bennett was kicking for goal, for touch, launching an attack, covering in defence; all were accomplished with the stamp of real class and authority – all his powers seemed to peak on this tour.

Yet for a man labelled as the 'world's best', Bennett had a very sticky time during the next season. His first son died just before the Wales-All Blacks game in November and the fly-half looked decidedly out of form. He was relegated to the Possibles for the Welsh trial and John Bevan was in his place for the first international. Bevan took his chance well, but lost his place when injured in the Scotland game; Bennett was back in control. The see-saw continued when a bruised foot necessitated him missing the game against Australia; Bevan's turn again and he was named for the game against England in 1976 with Dai Richards as his reserve. Bennett not even second best;

Llanelli reeled with indignation. But, according to Max Boyce, divine intervention took place; Bevan and Richards were unfit and the number 10 shirt was worn by Phil Bennett. It was his for the season—a Grand Slam season for Wales—and he was never again seriously threatened for his position in the national team. In addition, he captained Llanelli to their fourth WRU Cup in a row.

The Grand Slam game against France was the final international appearance of the world's top No. 8, Mervyn Davies, who had captained Wales in 1975 and 1976. Terry Cobner seemed to be the selectors' choice as a replacement when he was named to lead Wales in the unofficial Test against Argentina in October 1976 and then the Probables in the trial on New Year's Day, but the Pontypool man had been plagued by injuries during the season and it was the Llanelli fly-half who was given the honour of leading his country. With a Lions' tour at the end of the season, Bennett was immediately in the forefront of runners to captain that side, too. His main rival for the position was England's skipper Roger Uttley, whose side was in line for their first Triple Crown for 17 years when they travelled down to Cardiff. Both England's hopes of triumph and Uttley's hopes of leading the Lions disappeared at the Arms Park that day. And, as if to emphasise his position, Bennett scored the try of the season in the Triple Crown-winning performance against Scotland at Murrayfield. He finished off a 90-yard vintage move and clasping the ball, looking back down the pitch, the Llanelli fly-half seemed to have the Rugby world at his feet.

Bennett was duly elected to captain the British Lions on their tour of New Zealand, the side having high hopes of maintaining their supremacy in world terms. The All Blacks were in a transitional period and it was Jack Gleeson's first major series as coach. After the successes of the Lions in 1971 and 1974, there was a lot of pressure on this side, who had to contend with the wettest New Zealand winter for many, many years.

The British forwards were able to cope with these conditions and had a much greater domination over the All Blacks than the 1971 side ever had. But the backline never clicked, very rarely playing with the confidence associated with British backs, especially in New Zealand. Bennett, seemingly unsettled at having to come in to receive the shorter passes of Dougie Morgan and Brynmor Williams, never controlled as he had done in South Africa and he was not helped by a bad shoulder injury he sustained in the first Test. It was not the happiest of tours and, although the series was only narrowly lost, it was evident that the All Blacks could well have been beaten decisively.

The tour had taken a lot out of Bennett, mentally and physically, and he was glad when it was all over. Yet, with a short rest, he was back as captain of Wales, in his best form, and leading them to a second Grand Slam in three years. The summer of 1977 was behind him and he revelled again in the long pass of Gareth Edwards. And, in true captain's fashion, Bennett scored the two tries which ended the French challenge in the final match of the championship. It was not known at the time, but this was the farewell performance of Edwards and Bennett for Wales, either together or individually, as neither toured Australia in the summer and both announced their retirements at the beginning of the next season; Bennett's from international Rugby and Edwards' completely.

Bennett carried on captaining Llanelli, where his form was still of international standard; there could be no hiding his magnificent footballing abilities. This diminutive player in those red jerseys will long be remembered as the fly-half who emerged from the shadow of Barry John and became a giant in his own right, every bit as legendary as 'King John'.

Gordon Brown

Scottish second-row forward Gordon Brown played a major role in the success of the Lions on their three tours during the seventies. The environment of touring, especially with regard to training, brought out the best in this Ayrshire lock who needed that pressure to achieve peak fitness. From the raw, rather naive, cherubic-faced youngster who visited New Zealand in

Gordon Brown's coming-of-age tour – his visit to New Zealand with the 1971 Lions; here he stretches in a line-out against NZ Universities.

1971, Gordon Lamont Brown grew up along with the British forwards until the Lions' packs of 1974 and 1977 gained control never before envisaged. A knowledge of the basic techniques, plus a refusal to be intimidated, gave these forwards an authority never before realised. And Brown was very much the 'new breed' British forward in this respect. Always a fervent nationalist when playing—for Britain when wearing the Lions' red and for Scotland when in the blue jersey with the white thistle—he took immense pride in playing for Scotland and in being a Scottish member of the Lions' parties; 'Broon o' Troon' as he became known, was the symbol of the new-found pride in itself of British Rugby during the seventies.

An immensely strong mauler and scrummager, he also developed into a valuable middle-of-the-line jumper for the Lions. (This was a reversal of his Scottish role where Alastair McHarg was the main jumper with Gordon Brown at the front.) In front of Brown was, firstly, Willie John McBride and then England's Bill Beaumont. Brown's presence and weight were invaluable in scrums, rucks and mauls as he was able to rip the ball from opponents and set up quality possession. He was impressive in the loose on the 1974 Lions' tour in South Africa, where he scored eight tries including two in the Test series.

Despite this he has never scored in any of his thirty international appearances for Scotland. And more surprisingly, his last Scottish cap, up until the end of the 1978-79 season, was in March 1976, the day Scotland beat Ireland in Dublin. For the next three seasons he was not to pull on the blue jersey, a great source of disappointment to the player himself, especially at a time when Scotland needed him desperately. At one stage, it looked possible that Brown could become Scotland's most-capped player of all time, but there is doubt now about whether he will add to his total of thirty. It has been a bitter blow for Scottish Rugby,

because he was the perfect foil for the wayward genius of Alastair McHarg, whose wanderings could be tolerated as long as Brown, or someone of his size and style, was there to partner him. The pair complemented each other perfectly and recorded twenty-one internationals together for Scotland in the second-row.

Gordon Brown, born in Troon, Ayrshire in 1947, came from a very sporting background. His father, Jock, played soccer and kept goal for Scotland and Gordon's elder brother, Peter, was a Scotland Rugby international, captaining the side on many occasions. Before Gordon Brown's six-foot five and nearly seventeen-stone frame developed, the youngster played fly-half at Troon Primary. But by the time he left Marr College, having spent a season in the first team, he was well and truly ensconced in the pack. The next four years were in his FP's top fifteen, before trying his luck with West of Scotland in 1968. West had recently provided two international locks, but McHarg had gone to London Scottish and Gordon's brother Peter had left to play for Gala.

After a few injury problems, the young lock was chosen to tour Argentina with the national party the following summer. Because of an injury to Jim Telfer, McHarg was moved to No. 8 and Gordon Brown brought in to partner Peter Stagg in the second-row in the unofficial international. But Telfer was declared fit on the morning of the match and Brown was told that he would not be playing after all. It was an upsetting incident, but he did not have to wait long for his Scotland cap as he played in the victory over the Springboks in December 1969. The following year, Brown became the first player to replace his brother in an international and was now an established member of the Scotland team, part-

Gordon Brown—'Broon o' Troon'—was the only player to be selected for all three Lions' tours in the seventies.

nering the giant Peter Stagg in his first six games before teaming up with Alastair McHarg. The young lock made his first Lions' tour in 1971 and quickly grew up in the rough and tumble of New Zealand forward play. His form improved to such an extent that he forced Delme Thomas out of the Test pack for the final two internationals. Brown was replaced in the final game after some vicious early exchanges as the All Blacks tried unsuccessfully to save the series. Brown's reputation had grown rapidly because of his New Zealand performances and he was now a member of the hard core of the Scotland scrum along with Ian McLauchlan, Sandy Carmichael and Alastair McHarg. He was missing for most of the 1973 season through injury, and his brother Peter moved up to partner McHarg in the second-row. It was nearly a Triple Crown year for the Scots, but, although Brown came on as a replacement during the Calcutta Cup game, he could not save his side from conceding four tries and defeat at Twickenham.

The following year was an important one for Brown, playing some of his finest Rugby with the Lions in South Africa. He was the top try-scoring forward with eight in all, two of which were in the Tests. His try, just before half-time in the third Test when he crashed through at a line-out, brought up the thousandth point in internationals against South Africa. With a hand injury preventing him taking part in the final international, Brown had played in five Tests for the Lions with the enviable record of four wins and a draw.

Yet, when the lock walked off the park at Lansdowne Road in March 1976, there was no suggestion that he would not be wearing the Scottish jersey again in the decade. His problems began in December of that year when he was sent off for retaliation against the North and Midlands hooker Alan Hardie in Glasgow's inter-district game at Murrayfield. The SRU had promised severe punishments for misde-

meanours and Brown's case was not helped by the fact his fighting was done in front of the Murrayfield stand and before the television cameras. Brown was suspended for twelve weeks; the extent of his provocation can be judged from the fact that Hardie was banned for sixteen months. Those twelve weeks were an 'electric chair' sentence to a player who needs competitive Rugby to maintain his match-fitness.

Away from the game, he trained with Glasgow Rangers soccer club at Ibrox, where he was put through some very severe training sessions. It was all worth it however, because he was picked for his third consecutive Lions' tour, returning to New Zealand. Gordon Brown is the only player to have been selected for the initial party in every British Lions' tour during the seventies. After some early shoulder trouble, Brown made the side for the final three Tests, experiencing his first international defeats while playing for the Lions. Partnering Bill Beaumont, Brown helped the forwards establish a domination they never had in 1971. Unfortunately, the backs were not of the 1971 vintage and that control could not be converted into points. Still, Gordon Brown had maintained his habit of playing his best Rugby for the Lions, rising to the occasion and challenge of proving himself better than his southern hemisphere counterparts.

Back at Twickenham that September, playing for the British Lions against the Barbarians in the Queen's Silver Jubilee match, Brown's shoulder went again, and he was forced out of Rugby for a while. When the shoulder healed, his back went again and for varying reasons and injuries, Brown has been unable to take up his place in the Scotland scrum. Even if he does not return, the Troon man has more than played his part in the development of British forward play during the seventies, helping destroy for ever the mythology that surrounded the power of the All Black and Springbok packs.

Jeff Butterfield

How England have longed for a centre in the Butterfield style over the past twenty years; they have found no-one to replace him. The Lions have managed once or twice, with players like John Dawes and Mike Gibson, but even now their talents seem to be one of the rarest commodities to be found on a Rugby field. Butterfield had the qualities of a classic centre; he was elusive, quick on the break, intelligent and, above all, he was a beautiful passer of the ball. South Africa's Dr Danie Craven rates him the best running midfield back he has ever seen; he had first noted the centre's

promise when he saw the young twenty-one-year old appear for the North-East Counties against the visiting 1950-51 Springboks. It was to be over two years before Butterfield played for England and four years before South African crowds delighted at his performances with the Lions.

Jeffrey Butterfield was one of the earliest talents to appear from that well-known Rugby nursery, Loughborough Colleges, making his mark initially with Northampton and Yorkshire, then England and the Lions. After leading Yorkshire to their first success in the County Championship for a quarter of a century in 1953, he made his debut for England later that season against France. He could not have wished for a better start. Within a minute he had split the French defence open with an interception, sending Woodward away for a try; the debutant scored himself in the final seconds of the game to seal an 11-0 victory. 'Butterfield has come to stay' was the general agreement of the supporters and media alike.

His second international saw him partnered in the centre by a man whose name has become synonymous with his, Phil Davies. They are generally rated England's best pair of centres since the war, and some also think before it. They complemented each other perfectly, Butterfield providing the brain and Davies the brawn – to categorise their talents in the simplest form. In many ways, they would have been suited to the New Zealand style of playing a second five-eighth and one centre, with the inside man creating the opportunities for his hard-running partner.

They proved a fearsome combination, no more so than in South Africa in 1955, where they were able to carry on their England pairing for the Lions. Both Butterfield and Davies were vital members to the success of that party. The Yorkshireman rates the first

Jeff Butterfield demonstrates his finest midfield quality – the supposedly simple task of passing the ball.

Test, which saw the Lions scrape home 23-22 after being 23-11 ahead, as the greatest game he ever played in. Certainly there can have been few more nail-biting climaxes to an international. Butterfield and Davies were made all the more dangerous by Cliff Morgan's presence at fly-half. Butterfield and the dynamic Welshman had a perfect understanding; both were instinctive players and with Morgan varying his passes and Butterfield's clever running off the ball, they created all sorts of havoc in defences all over South Africa on that tour. The trio were split up in the fourth Test when Davies was dropped. A move, in retrospect, which may have cost the Lions the chance of winning the series instead of drawing it.

Butterfield was probably at his finest on that tour; the grounds were perfectly suited to running and the centre delighted the crowds as well as his own side with masterful displays. Tony O'Reilly, for one, has reason to be grateful to the English pair for many of his sixteen tries. Butterfield himself scored many fine efforts, with his best-remembered being in the game against Northern Transvaal. With the Lions forwards down to seven men, they were defending stoutly, but had seen their lead dwindle until the home side were level, 11-11. But, in the circumstances, a draw was a good result against one of South Africa's strongest provincial sides. As the game entered the final minute, it seemed as though the Lions had managed to hold out.

But some of the Lions' backs had different ideas and, true to character, Cliff Morgan was one of them. When he received the ball behind his own line from a scrum, he did not make the expected kick to touch. Instead, he broke to the '25' where he lobbed a long pass to Butterfield, who had Davies and Pedlow outside him. Ahead was the Northern Transvaal full-back, Gayer, but with a two-man overlap, the centre had only to draw his man. This he did, but suddenly swerved inside him, leaving a sixty-yard race for the line. No-one was going to catch him and he dived by the posts to give the Lions one of their finest victories.

Another of his highlights on that tour was unique, for him at least. With the score at 0-0 just before half-time in the third Test, he gathered a loose ball and calmly dropped a left-footed goal. Unique, yes; it was his first dropped goal in representative Rugby and only one of two in his whole career! He added a try in the second half, helping the Lions to a 2-1 lead in the series, which was eventually drawn. Butterfield returned from South Africa rated as one of the greatest players ever to have visited those shores.

Butterfield continued playing for England, although Phil Davies was not always there to partner him in the centre, and in 1959 the Yorkshireman captained England in the international campaign. They drew their games with Scotland and France, lost to Wales, beat Ireland and in the four games scored nine points against eleven (the high-scoring games in the championships of the seventies were still a long way off). During his England career, Butterfield had won two Triple Crowns in 1954 and 1957, the second also being a Grand Slam, and in addition to those years, England also won the championship in 1953 and 1958. It was a golden era for English Rugby and Jeff Butterfield's niche as a guiding force in this period is assured.

The year of his captaincy also saw him make his second tour with the British Lions, this time to Australasia. He had not been playing well for England during the season, but felt that the atmosphere and environment of being on tour would help him to recapture his old form and provide a grand finale to his career. But it was not to be; an injury in Australia, then a more serious one in New Zealand followed by the recurrence of a damaged thigh muscle which had plagued him during his career, saw to that. It was a sad end as he still had much to offer the side and a vintage Butterfield would have been a perfect foil for young Dave Hewitt.

Mike Gibson suffered the same problem on the Lions' tour to New Zealand in 1977; in both cases, a fit Butterfield or Gibson might have made all the difference.

His philosophy on Rugby was: 'This is a wonderful game – difficult to understand and not all that easy to play. Everything is there to satisfy the individual, but it demands fitness and boldness in play if one is to obtain full value, elation and satisfaction.' Jeff Butterfield provided all those things and he brought a rare talent to England's midfield that has been sadly lacking ever since.

All eyes on Ken Catchpole's fly-half as he passes out for the Wallabies against Ebbw Vale & Abertillery in 1966.

Ken Catchpole

The finest Rugby player produced by Australia since the war, Ken Catchpole was arguably the best scrum-half of his period. From his international debut in 1961 – in which he also captained the Wallabies – until his career was abruptly ended in an incident with Colin Meads in 1968, Kenneth William Catchpole consistently proved himself a footballer of outstanding ability. He was a player with all the skills, harnessed by a shrewd tactical awareness that would almost instinctively take the correct option. Catchpole was slick, fast, intuitive and played with a lot of style; there was no one aspect of his game that could be

described as better than the rest. Although his passing did not have the extraordinary length of a mature Gareth Edwards, it was still lightning quick and deadly accurate, giving his three-quarters plenty of time in which to move the ball. There was an exceptional balance and poise about his running

A dive pass from Ken Catchpole on the 1963 Australian tour of South Africa. The Wallabies shocked the Springboks by drawing the series, 2-2.

with the ball, that air of apparent ease that suggests that Rugby is fundamentally a simple game to play. And if running with the ball failed to bring points, then his kicking would probe for the gaps he knew existed somewhere. His game revolved around the appearance of the minimum of effort and Catchpole certainly fitted the description, a graceful player.

Ken Catchpole was born in Sydney in 1939 and his schoolboy Rugby was played

for Coogee Prep and Scot's College. He made the Sydney representative schools side and was also a notable athlete. In his first season of senior Rugby, the scrum-half made the Randwick (Sydney) first fifteen and the New South Wales side. He made his mark immediately, scoring a try and performing expertly against Dickie Jeeps, when New South Wales beat Ronnie Dawson's 1959 British Lions. The newcomer's reputation was established and

after leading Australia in three unofficial Tests against the Fijians he was selected to tour South Africa in 1961 as captain of the Wallabies. His international debut, as captain as well as scrum-half, was not a happy occasion as the Springboks won 28-3 to record their biggest-ever victory over Australia. But even that hammering could not hide the promise of the new five foot six, ten and a half stone scrum-half, who had skippered his country at the age of only 21.

Two years later, Catchpole teamed up with Phil Hawthorne in a partnership that became regarded as the best in the world and the half backs played a large part in the Wallabies' revenging that early defeat by the Springboks. By now, Catchpole had lost the captaincy to John Thornett, but was still continuing to control from scrum-half. After losing the first Test, the Australians went on to win the next two before eventually sharing the series. Another name linked with Catchpole's at the time, almost as closely as that of Hawthorne's, was Greg Davis on the flank. Catchpole utilised Davis's destructive ability as effectively as Hawthorne's creativity. It was an era when Australian Rugby regained its pride and became a world force again. For this, much of the credit must go to Ken Catchpole. As well as his individual ability, he brought out the best of those around him, giving them increased confidence and the opportunity to play at the top of their game.

By the time he came to Britain with John Thornett's side in 1966, Ken Catchpole's reputation had long preceded him to the northern hemisphere Rugby countries. He was the world's number one scrum-half, but still had to prove it in front of the British supporters. This he did masterfully and is generally accepted as probably the finest footballing scrum-half to have visited these shores. His pairing with Hawthorne was at its peak, controlling those international victories over Wales and England; and in the latter game Hawthorne also dropped three goals. Their career together was near-

ing its end, however, with Hawthorne turning to Rugby league after the 1967 game against the All Blacks.

So Catchpole played without his fly-half partner of so many internationals in the 1968 game against the All Blacks. Little did the scrum-half know that this was to be his final game for his country. In his twenty-fourth international, the Wallaby scrum-half found himself trapped in a ruck with one leg protruding, the other trapped. Colin Meads, in an effort to get at the ball, grabbed the loose leg and heaved. Catchpole was performing an involuntary splits and when the leg would go no further, the leg muscles tore; his international career had been ripped away. Meads' motives were questioned and for one with so much international experience, his action was rather clumsy. The All Black lock was apologetic, but it was fact that one of Australia's finest footballers would play no more. It was an inauspicious end to a glorious career. Luckily for Australia, they are in the habit of producing excellent scrum-halves. Catchpole's understudy on that 1966-67 British tour, John Hipwell, now proved more than an adequate successor.

Ken Catchpole was a legend in his own time; his exemplary attitude to the game and his behaviour to colleague and opponent like only increased the esteem in which he was held. He was a natural who did not waste his talent; and, moreover, used his skills for the good of the team and those he played with. He had rare gifts, but was more than willing to share them with us all.

Don Clarke

The greatest match-winner in the history of Rugby football, Don Clarke's influence was such that many would have changed the laws to have reduced the effectiveness of this one full-back from New Zealand. From the 1956 series against the Springboks until

Don Clarke, whose boot was Rugby's greatest match-winner, pictured after his retirement but wearing once again his All Black jersey.

the 1963-64 All Blacks' tour of Britain and France, his boot dominated the international scene – a period unparalleled in the pressure cauldron of top-class Rugby.

It was a period of consistency and power that can be best summed up by eighty minutes' Rugby on July 18, 1959, a date Clarke describes as thus: 'What a day that was. Within the span of a few hours I felt the greatest pride of my career, at least up to then, followed by a feeling of genuine disgust. Both reactions stemmed from the actions of the British Lions then on tour in New Zealand. That was a day of penalties, records – and flying oyster shells, jelly, and hot tempers.'

The match was the first Test between the All Blacks and the British Lions, and few internationals have prompted so much discussion and controversy. It was not because the New Zealanders had won by a single point, but rather the manner of their victory. Those 1959 Lions were a talented side with backs like O'Reilly, Jackson and Risman capable of tearing apart the toughest defence. And the New Zealanders in that opening game proved no great obstacle as the British side ran in four tries. In reply, the All Blacks managed eighteen points . . . without crossing the visitors' line! The hero, or in some circles the villain, was Donald Barrie Clarke, who kicked six penalty goals in difficult conditions. The Lions had led 17-9 with less than a quarter of an hour to go, but Clarke doubled his tally of penalty goals and points to emerge as the central figure in a famous All Black victory.

But those four tries to none had turned the game into a moral victory for the British side, although they would have surely preferred the win in the record books. And the unfortunate Clarke's six penalty goals had turned the goal-kicker into some kind of a monster who was ruining the game of Rugby; a feeling not lost on Clarke himself, as he recalls: 'This match has been used to build up an image of me as some vaguely unhealthy influence on the game.' Don

Clarke felt, of course, that the criticism was unfair. He was merely making the most of opportunities presented to him through the game. These kind of opportunities had first brought him to the notice of the New Zealand public eight years previously.

Born in Taranaki in 1933, he always had a build beyond his years and it was no surprise when he was brought into the Waikato provincial side at the age of 17. In only his seventh game, he kicked two penalty goals from the surface of a swamp to bring Waikato their first Ranfurly Shield as they defeated North Auckland 6-3. Warning had been given of the promise of this young full-back and, although it was to be five years before he made his debut for his country, New Zealanders were already talking about Don Clarke, a player who was to become a legend long before he retired from the international scene. Two of the next four seasons were spent having the cartilages removed from his knees, but by 1956 he was ready to bid for the spot at the rear of the New Zealand defence.

The All Blacks had won the first and lost the second Test in the series against the Springboks; obviously changes were to be made for the third match. Clarke had already played a significant part in helping Waikato defeat the visiting South Africans in the opening game of their tour and it was to him the New Zealand selectors turned for the third Test. Also in the side was Don Clarke's brother Ian, and they became the first set of brothers to play for the All Blacks since Cyril and Maurice Brownlie turned out against France in 1925.

Within sixteen minutes the home side were 11-0 in front and Clarke had marked his debut with two penalty goals and a conversion. New Zealand won, 'The Boot' had arrived and the New Zealand public had found a new 'god'. No praise was too high for this youngster who had given the All Blacks a lead in the series, especially as he repeated his scoring act in the final Test to give his side a 3-1 advantage and their

Don Clarke, scourge of the British Lions in 1959, dives over for the last-minute try which won the second Test for the All Blacks.

first win in a series over the Springboks since 1937.

Both Australia and the Lions were to feel the weight and power of his boot before the decade was out. In a twelve-match trip to Australia in 1957, he scored 163 points, including New Zealand's first goal from a mark since 1930. Two years later came that eventful series against the British Lions. His seemingly personal vendetta against that side did not end with his six penalty goals in the opening Test. He may have hung them in that game, but he waited until

the second and third matches before having the opposition drawn and quartered. Seldom has one man controlled the destiny of a Rugby series as Clarke did in 1959. One minute remained in the second Test and it seemed as though Ronnie Dawson's men had extracted their revenge. Ironically, the visitors were trailing two tries to one, but were leading 8-6, courtesy of a John Young try, converted by Terry Davies, who also kicked a penalty goal. Don Clarke's name was not on the scoresheet; surely a rare enough occurrence to warn the Lions' defence to keep an eye on this six-foot-two, sixteen-and-a-half-stone farmer. The game was in the final minute when the All Blacks won a ruck near the opposition line and scrum-half McCullough went blind; full-back Clarke was with him and he took the ball to run the final ten yards before hurling himself through the air to give New Zealand victory. He added the conversion for good measure.

The New Zealanders won the third Test more convincingly, 22-8, but it was that man Clarke who had again broken the deadlock. He kicked a fifty-yard penalty goal and dropped a left-footed goal in the space of a couple of minutes in the first half. It was enough to move the score from 3-3 to 9-3 and the All Blacks' pack, gathering inspiration from their full-back, forged ahead.

How the Lions must have loathed the sight of Don Clarke as he lined up a penalty attempt five minutes from time in the fourth and final Test. The visitors had scored three tries, but had missed all their kicks; Clarke already had two penalties under his belt and his goal-kicking meant that his side were only three points adrift. So, when Haydn Morgan fell offside on his own 25-yard line, fifteen yards in from touch and Clarke moved up to take the kick that would level the scores, it seemed there was no escape for British Rugby from the boot of this points-scoring phenomenon. But, to the surprise of Clarke, and probably to the greater surprise of the red-shirted players behind the goal, he hooked the ball badly. The Lions had won their first international in New Zealand since 1930. But the series belonged to New Zealand, and Clarke in particular. Without his 39 points, there is little doubt that the All Blacks would have been beaten.

His reputation was now world-wide and his performances the following year in South Africa made him the game's number one personality. He scored one hundred and seventy-five points on the tour (two hundred and ten including the Australian part) and, as with the Lions, there was a time when he threatened to win the Test series off his own boot. The Springboks had dominated the first Test – even giving Clarke his first blank scoresheet in internationals – but had lost the second when a left-footed dropped goal by the huge full-back brought him his century of test points in only a dozen games.

The next game between the two countries is rated as one of Clarke's finest matches. All had seemed lost for the New Zealanders when they trailed 3-11 with six minutes remaining. Don Clarke reduced the deficit with a penalty goal from inside his own half. It gave New Zealand the hope to keep pressuring and in the dying minutes McMullen sprinted past Antelme to score five yards in from touch. The conversion would draw the game and keep the series wide open. As before, 'The Boot' did not fail his country when it needed him and his joy as the kick went over was only matched by the delight of one of the touch-judges as he signalled the points – it was Don's brother Ian. There was talk that Clarke was transforming a good side into a great one and that the All Blacks were gearing their play to using their full-back's kicking talents as much as possible. Captain Wilson Whineray was quick to point out that you play to your strengths in Rugby, and in terms of that, there is little doubt that Clarke was on a par with Samson!

Although even his presence was not enough to prevent the Springboks winning the final Test and the series, on a personal level the tour was a tremendous triumph for the full-back. His goal-kicking had been immaculate, as had his play around the field. He was easily the most popular and sought-after member of the touring party and the adulation of the South African public reached the heights of hero-worship. Without him, it is difficult to see how the All Blacks could have made a contest of it in the Tests.

The only major Rugby-playing country which had not yet felt the full impact of his boot was France; but that was put right in 1961 with what some have described as his greatest kick. The All Blacks had established a 1-0 lead in the series, but there was some doubt about the second Test taking place at Wellington. A gale had blown up on the morning of the match, with the 80-mile-an-hour gusts enough to prevent the liner *Canberra* from berthing at Wellington on her maiden voyage.

Eventually, the NZRFU gave the go-ahead and France decided to take advantage of the gale in the first half; but the All Black defence held out and there was no score before the interval. Amazingly, in the second half France took a 3-0 lead with a Dupuy try into the fierce wind. This spurred New Zealand on and Kel Tremain crossed ten yards in from touch. Clarke describes his attempt to kick the conversion in terrible conditions. 'The wind was roaring like a cyclone at my back as I placed the ball, aiming it at the corner flag. I moved in and kicked it, watching in wonder as the wind flung the ball between the uprights. It would be nice to take the credit which I've been given for that kick, described by some as "the greatest of all time." No, the kick was an absolute fluke. No-one could have judged that hurricane.'

Fluke or not, 'The Boot' had lived up to his ever-increasing reputation. In five years of international Rugby, he had scored one hundred and forty points from his seventeen appearances. Clarke had dominated proceedings from the minute he stepped on the international field. It is doubtful whether New Zealand would have won as many as thirteen of these games if Clarke had not been playing. Still, he was far from finished stabbing the ball through opposition posts and one effort against Australia in 1962 was measured seventy-two yards from kick to pitch . . . a mammoth effort, which was more than enough to silence jeers from the Sydney 'Hill'.

The following year brought more controversy; this time in the two-match series against England in New Zealand. Clarke had a successful opening international – scoring in all four possible ways. And, when Don and Ian Clarke ran onto Lancaster Park in the second game, they set a new record of twenty-four international appearances for New Zealand. This was a much harder game for the All Blacks. The score was 6–6 when the full-back made a mark on half-way, towards the left touchline. He retired eight yards with his brother holding the ball as he attempted to kick the goal which would give New Zealand victory. Clarke always took a steadying pace before starting his run up. At this movement, the England forwards charged, but the referee ruled that the charge was illegal and they were not allowed to move when Clarke took his kick. Without needing to worry about those forwards bearing down on him, Clarke was able to add the points that gave the All Blacks victory. Accusations were made that the New Zealander had deliberately provoked the opposition into moving, knowing that he could then take the kick unhurriedly. Probably at worst, Don Clarke was guilty of gamesmanship, rather like a scrum-half going on a dummy run in order to try and trap the opposing flankers offside.

Whatever the rights or wrongs of the situation, there was no doubt that Clarke was again the saviour. In all his record-breaking appearances for his country, his goal-kicking talents had never let him down for any considerable length of time.

Now he was to embark on his first major tour of Britain and France under the leadership of Whineray with his reputation as a match-winner having reached legendary proportions. But that tour was to bring him the first crisis in his playing and kicking career – so much so that for the final Test against France, he was relieved of his kicking duties. That was a situation which would have been considered unthinkable when the party left the New Zealand shores.

All had gone according to plan when the tour started and, by mid-tour, he seemed well on his way to 200 points plus. But he pulled a groin muscle in the Welsh Test in attempting to kick a seventy-yard goal. That kick missed and it signalled a run of failures that was to continue until near the end of the tour. The more he practised, the worse it became.

For a man whose philosophy up to then had been: 'If you miss, you miss; and any failure means that you have not hit the ball correctly', the loss of form must have been alarming, not helped by the varying opinions on what was wrong. He was even ordered not to practise at one stage. Perhaps the pressure was even greater because he had been successful for so long. Every top athlete experiences unexplained losses of form at one time or another . . . and Clarke had had a much longer run than most. Clarke was now soul searching on a technique of kicking that had served him and New Zealand faithfully for so long. This self-analysis was not helped by the fact that, at thirty, he was nearing the end of his career. Perhaps the loss of form was a signal to think of calling it a day.

But there was an unexpected bonus during this kicking lapse. The question that at last was being asked was: 'Without his goal-kicking, how good a full-back is this man Clarke?' It was about time that his general play emerged from the shadow of his boots. While not a top-notch player to compare with Bob Scott, he was no slouch around the field. His positional play was instinctive and he had the ability to clear enormous distances with either foot. For a big man, he was very mobile and he was very much a natural footballer, commanding a tremendous presence when at the back of the All Blacks' defence. He certainly proved an intimidatory influence on opposing sides during his reign.

Clarke's boot was still good enough to win the Irish Test and kick vital goals against Wales and England; so, it was only by his high, almost unattainable standards that he was considered a failure. He admits that, after those years of unbroken success and responsibility a kicker carries, he was ill-prepared for a change of fortune. When his form did return, Clarke compared it to one of those sweaty nightmares you wake from in a flash. At last 'The Boot' was back, finishing the tour in grand style by kicking six conversions out of eight against the Barbarians.

It was only right that he should find his touch before returning to New Zealand . . . lest the British public should be in any doubt about his great talent. He was to play only two more matches for the All Blacks, against Australia in 1964, before knee trouble forced him to retire. It is sad that Clarke's last game should end in defeat – it was only his fourth in thirty-one outings for New Zealand. But his two hundred and one points in international Rugby have assured him a place as New Zealand's and Rugby's greatest match-winner.

Fran Cotton

Talented prop Fran Cotton can play on either side of the scrum with equal success. His performances at tight-head on the 1974 Lions' tour and those at loose-head in New Zealand in 1977 were of the highest quality, establishing him as an obvious contender for any world fifteen during the seventies.

The British Lions' front row for the final three Tests in New Zealand in 1977. From left : Graham Price, Peter Wheeler and Fran Cotton.

Tall for a prop—six foot two—Cotton developed his talents at an early age, first capped for England at twenty-three. By the time of his first British Lions' tour, he was already rated as one of the world's best. Exceptionally powerful, Cotton used his sixteen and a half stone to good effect in ruck and maul alike and was very prominent around the field. Of the two prop positions, he thought he was too tall for loose-head, where he felt a smaller man with the same strength had better leverage, and that he was better suited to tight-head.

Fran Cotton feeds the ball to Peter Dixon during England's game against Wales at the Arms Park in 1977, when the home side ended England's Triple Crown hopes.

Born in Wigan in 1948, Francis (later known as Fran) Edward Cotton was brought up in a Rugby League background. Not only the locality; his father had been a League international for England. At Newton-le-Willows grammar school, the youngster developed as a hooker, but soon grew too big and moved along the front-row to prop. After school and a period with Liverpool, Cotton went to study at one of Britain's great Rugby nurseries, Loughborough Colleges. And it was from there that he received his first international honours. After three matches as a travelling reserve, he made his debut in the 1971 Calcutta Cup game. That was lost, as were his other two games that year, but he was

selected to go with the national side to the Far East. It was not a successful tour and Cotton was left out the following season. His recovery began when he went with England to South Africa in 1972 and, although he was squeezed out of the Test place by Mike Burton, he was back in favour and soon teamed up with 'Stack' Stevens and John Pullin; the trio were to play ten internationals together.

In the 1972-73 season Fran Cotton captained England to victory in the International Sevens played at Murrayfield as part of Scotland's centenary celebrations. That season was a time of great triumph for the England prop. Not only did he play his way back into the national side, but also captained the North-West Counties side that beat Kirkpatrick's team (the first time that an English regional team had ever beaten the All Blacks) and led Loughborough Colleges to victory in the UAU Championship. If that was not enough, he was a member of the Lancashire fifteen that won the County Championship; then in the summer of 1973, Cotton took his place at prop when England beat the All Blacks for the first time in New Zealand. It was in the southern hemisphere that Cotton played some of his finest Rugby. He respected their forward power and saw them as the ultimate challenge.

Cotton was an automatic choice for the 1974 Lions and was one of the magnificent eight in the pack which steam-rollered Springbok forwards all over South Africa. The front-row (with Cotton at tight-head) consisted of a Scotsman, a Welshman and an Englishman – Ian McLauchlan and Bobby Windsor packing down with Cotton. The three became one of the attractions of the tour, great favourites with the crowds, if not always with their opposing front-rows.

Back home he was appointed captain of England, but injury finished his reign almost before it began. By now his regular hooker was Leicester's Peter Wheeler. In Cotton's twenty-five appearances, up until

the end of the 1978-79 season, he only packed down with two hookers for England –John Pullin (thirteen times) and Peter Wheeler (twelve times). His other props were 'Piggy' Powell (twice), 'Stack' Stevens (twelve times), Mike Burton (five times), Robin Cowling (four times) and Barry Nelmes (twice). After three years with Coventry, Cotton joined Sale in 1975.

The seventies were not a very successful period for England's national side, but Cotton, with the rest of the front-row, never let the side down and usually gave them an advantage the backs never utilised. By the time he was selected for his second Lions' tour, in 1977, Cotton was one of the senior professionals and helped form another memorable front-row combination. This time Cotton was at loose-head with Graham Price at tight and Peter Wheeler hooking. As with England, the forwards dominated and the battles were won, but the war was lost. It was a feeling that Cotton had experienced many times before when playing for England. It would have been with great difficulty that he tried to visualise the days when, with only about a quarter possession, British backs had used their meagre rations to run the All Blacks ragged.

Injury problems dogged him when he returned home, missing two internationals in the 1978 championship and hardly playing at all the following season. The All Blacks, led by Graham Mourie, visited in late 1978 and Cotton would dearly have loved a chance to have another crack at them, but disappointingly had to sit out their games against the North and England. He was not to appear again that season and was still missing when the England party to tour the Far East was named. Yet, after eight years of international Rugby, Fran Cotton was still a very necessary part of England's plans. Props of his calibre are very rare. He returned to the international scene against the All Blacks in November 1979.

Fran Cotton attacks the French in the 1973 international at Twickenham, the scene of England's first win over the Tricolours for four years.

Michel Crauste

A flanker, Michel Crauste was one of the most respected and feared forwards on the Rugby scene in the first half of the sixties. An iron-hard player, there was little missing from this Frenchman's repertoire . . . whether in attack or defence. Crauste, with the ball in his hands, was always a danger, threading his way through defences more in the manner of a wing or a centre. And if Crauste did not have the ball, then he would not be far away from the man who did, scoring many tries with his expert positioning and timing in support. If you had the ball, then Michel Crauste would be one of the players you would least like to see bearing down, especially if colleagues and space were scarce. His tackles were as devastating as those bursts on the attack. Sometimes his commitment would lead him into the narrow area between late and dangerous tackles and he was often accused of over-robust play, but the Frenchman believed in total dedication to Rugby and his team's cause and those incidents were just a part of the game.

During his reign as captain of his country, Crauste led by example, bullying and cajolling his charges into greater efforts and to follow him as he took the game to the enemy. And those French team-mates had no better example to follow; but it was often felt, even in France, that the diplomacy and psychology of captaincy was missing from Crauste's make-up. Some even thought him tactically weak, courageously leading France out of desperate situations that he had led them into in the first place. Yet, there was no denying his commitment to the game; his appetite for Rugby, as it was for the ball and the defenders who held on to it, was insatiable. His style of perpetual motion was as familiar to the Rugby public as was his appearance. His shallow, withdrawn, almost ghostly complexion plus the ever-present moustache were his hallmarks and earned him the nicknames of 'Attila' and 'The Mongol'. No French team in the early sixties would have been complete without his name—his courage and skill providing a combination that earned Crauste and French forwards respect in all the major Rugby-playing countries.

Perhaps the highspot of his career was leading the Tricolours on their tour of South Africa in 1964. Crauste inspired his team to an 8-6 win in the only Test. It made up for his disappointment in not being able

Michel Crauste gets his pass away despite the attentions of England wing Jim Roberts. Crauste scored three tries against England in one afternoon at Colombes in 1962.

ment than his standard of play. Crauste was criticised in and out of France for his over-vigorous play, quite severely on the 1961 French tour of New Zealand where there were feelings that his zealous play sometimes contradicted the spirit in which Rugby should be played.

But players born in the south-west of France have never been noted for their delicacy of combat on the Rugby field and Michel Crauste, born in 1934, was no exception. And this flanker, just under six foot and weighing over thirteen and a half stone, proved an instant success when he burst upon the 1958 international championship and would have been a certain choice for the South African tour, but he was unavailable to go. Crauste achieved the notable feat of winning the French club championship in successive years with different clubs. In 1959, he was playing for the Racing Club de France while studying in Paris as an electrical technician when they won the title. The following year, he was turning out for Lourdes when they won the championship. He was to remain with Lourdes for the rest of his career, captaining them for much of that time.

And it was not only the club championship that he excelled in. At international level, there were outright wins for France in 1959, 1961 and 1962 and a shared title with England in 1960. And although Crauste came under criticism on that 1961 tour to New Zealand, he was one of the successes of the tour with the All Blacks and their supporters confirming Crauste's world-class status as France's top forward. Crauste was to play a full part in France's nine international years from 1958, and for most of those seasons was their outstanding forward. He was certainly not the favourite opponent of fly-halves who were playing for England, Scotland, Ireland and

to visit that country with the French party six years earlier, when France again won the series under Celaya who was one of six captains that Crauste played under before he himself took over: the others were Mias, Barthe, Moncla, Lacroix and Fabre. The long wait is put down more to his tempera-

Wales during his career. He was unmercifully uncompromising in his attitude and play, having by now created a reputation that would have ensured a place in any world fifteen. His final eleven appearances for France were as captain, his major achievement in that field being the victory in South Africa where they defeated the Springboks 8-6. France were denied the championship in his final year, 1966, when they went down 9-8 to Wales in the last game; Stuart Watkins scoring one of the great tries at Cardiff by running seventy-five yards with ten minutes to go. In the last seconds Lacaze missed a penalty chance that would have given France the title.

Crauste announced his retirement at the end of the season, having made 62 appearances in a French jersey, 43 (39 on the flank and four at No. 8) of those against major Rugby-playing countries which was then a record for his country. Many thought that Michel Crauste had retired prematurely and his departure left a gaping hole on the French flank. He will always be remembered for his dedication to the French game and the name of Crauste will always be associated with a marauding forward. His finest individual performance was probably his display against England at Colombes in 1962 in the home side's 13-0 victory, with Crauste adding three tries to his normal all-energy play on the flank. French Rugby matured during the late fifties and the early sixties through the influence of players like Mias, Prat and Michel Crauste. Without Crauste, French Rugby might have taken just that bit longer to grow up.

Benoit Dauga

A talented forward, Benoit Dauga spent his international career at lock and No. 8. His reign spanned almost a decade and he retired with fifty caps against International Board countries, a record for France, achieving his half-century quicker than any other of Rugby's fifty-cap winners. Dauga played against the best all over the world and won respect for his consistent performances. Frik du Preez, the Springbok, went as far as to rate the Frenchman as the finest forward he ever played against. When you realise that du Preez was also contemporary with Colin Meads, Willie John McBride and Walter Spanghero, it gives a measure of the esteem in which Dauga was held.

Later in his career, Spanghero and Dauga were often in conflict and there were worries about playing them in the same French side. It was a great blow to France as the pair were two of the finest forwards they have ever produced. But when Dauga broke his neck in a club game which left him temporarily paralysed, it was Walter Spanghero, his old adversary, who travelled to be at his bedside. Neither could deny the other's contribution to Rugby.

Dauga was usually in control at the line-out, earning himself nicknames of 'The Eiffel Tower', 'The Oxygen Bag' and 'Control Tower'. And, despite his six-foot-five and sixteen-stone frame, he was remarkably agile and quick around the park. He had the hands and poise of a three-quarter and was one of the most constructive forwards ever produced by France.

This mobility plus a natural toughness and robustness made him a difficult man to contain, especially when devoted to the cause of French Rugby, though this involvement could lead to problems: 'Once, when I was dropped for a supposed loss of form, I remained at home and watched the telecast of the match with friends. When the French team trotted on to the field, something gripped me and I burst into tears. The thought that I could be so sentimental has embarrassed me. Sentimentality can lead to complications and I dislike them.' Not that many of his opponents would have thought he was prone to such feelings; he was an uncompromising, no-nonsense opponent on the field.

Benoît Dauga leaps high in the line-out, despite the attentions of Ireland's Mick Hipwell in the 1971 game.

Born in Montgaillard in 1942, the young Dauga was brought up on a farm in the south-west of France. His early allegiances were to basketball and he only switched to Rugby at the age of eighteen. At the time of his move, many wondered whether he had the physical capabilities to survive on the Rugby field. He began with the Saint-Sever club before joining the Army for his national service. Dauga put in a superb performance for the French Forces against their British counterparts and established himself as a strong contender for the national side. When demobbed, he joined Mont-de-Marsan, a club that had the considerable talents of André Boniface.

Dauga made his debut against Scotland in 1964 and played six times for France that year, all in the second row, including the 8-6 victory over the Springboks on the tour of South Africa. The lock had impressed immediately in his introduction into the international scene, with his line-out skills and his mobility around the field rated as his strongest points. Dauga partnered Walter Spanghero during the following international season, but 1966 found the Mont-de-Marsan player at No. 8 in the French side for the first time. Although the majority of his caps were won in the second row, he was at his most dangerous and influential in the middle of the backrow of the scrum. And a part of the trouble between Dauga and Spanghero is revealed when the latter asserted: 'It does no service to Dauga to make him No. 8. He is better as a lock.' With Dauga as a lock, Spanghero would be able to continue his career as No. 8. But with Dauga at No. 8, and eventually captain, the Narbonne forward had to content himself with fitting in where possible, normally in the second row.

The French national team had a heavy fixture list towards the end of the late sixties with major tours to South Africa in 1967 and New Zealand in 1968, before entertaining the Springboks at the end of that year. Not one of these nine internationals was won by France. Many, including some of the players (Dauga was amongst this group), were critical of the fixture-arranging and the selectorial inconsistencies. France played nineteen internationals in 1967 and 1968, putting far too much strain on the top players. Yet Dauga's individual performances in South Africa and New Zealand had brought high praise from crowds who recognised a first-class forward when they saw one, especially rating his jumping in the line-out.

Despite falling to the southern hemisphere Rugby giants, Dauga played an essential part in France's championship in 1968, their first-ever Grand Slam. It was France's second championship in succession and they went on to share the title with Wales two years later. The Frenchman was given the captaincy of his country from No. 8 the following year for two matches before Carrère returned to the side. Later that year, he skippered one of the Tests against South

Benoit Dauga feeds Max Barrau in the 1971 England-France game at Twickenham. The French player on Dauga's right is his old adversary, Walter Spanghero.

Africa and led France in both internationals against Australia. The visit to South Africa was his third tour there. Dr Danie Craven, who was averse to mentioning individuals in a team game, had to salute Dauga as one of the greatest players ever seen in South Africa.

Dauga led France for the first three internationals in 1972 before being replaced as No. 8 and captain by Walter Spanghero. Although it did not seem possible at the time, his fifty-cap career was at an end. But his name cropped up in the news again when he broke his neck in a club game in 1975. He suffered a fractured dislocation of the neck, which led to damage to the spinal cord and paralysis. Fortunately, his determination to survive and the resilience he had shown many times on the field led to an almost total recovery. He is still involved in French Rugby today as a selector of the national side and his contribution is as valuable as his playing performances were. The worries that he would be unable to cope with the physical pressure of Rugby were proved groundless on many occasions, all over the Rugby world.

Gerald Davies

Welsh wing Gerald Davies was the game's most exciting runner in the seventies. Initially a midfield player, he developed into one of the most thrilling attractions Rugby has ever produced. His deadly acceleration and devastating sidesteps and jinks were difficult to counter; even among international players he was revered as something special. It was not that his eleven and a half stone frame was strong enough to break through tackles, instead his sidesteps were so severe and showed such a change of direction that would-be tacklers were lucky to get near enough even to touch him. And knowledge of his style was no real help . . . defenders knew what he was capable of, but there was little they could do to prevent him scoring.

Gerald Davies was an exceptional creator for Cardiff, London Welsh, Loughborough Colleges, Cambridge University, the Barbarians, Wales and the British Lions. His abilities and powers did not fade with age;

at the age of thirty-two, the wing dominated proceedings during the Sam Doble memorial game in 1977. The ability to beat defenders almost at will is rare and is one which Davies did not abuse. He was very much a favourite of crowds everywhere; they would will the ball out to him on the wing and you could sense expectation in the crowd increase when the finest runner in the game gained possession of the ball.

His defence improved as his career continued. He gave it the same consideration given to all his Rugby; Davies was a man who took his Rugby very seriously and was a deep thinker about the game. He was committed, especially as captain of Cardiff, to fifteen-man Rugby, involving all his players so they could provide a fitting spectacle for crowds everywhere.

Born in Llansaint near Kidwelly in February 1945, Thomas Gerald Reames Davies played for the Welsh Secondary Schools in 1963 before going to Loughborough Colleges. At this time he was looked upon as potentially one of the best centres in the country. In 1966, he made his debut for Wales in the same game as Barry John, and partnered John Dawes in the centre. Unfortunately, his debut day was spoilt by the Wallabies, who won 14-11. The rest of that season was spent alongside Billy Raybould in the national midfield. While showing the promise of being something special, Davies was thought of as rather indisciplined in his running and apt to make errors in his judgement. Still, his potential was real enough and, after playing in the centre with Keith Jarrett, he was selected to tour with the British Lions in South Africa in 1968. It was a frustrating tour for him. One of the British side's most dangerous attackers, first torn ligaments and then a dislocated elbow meant he was fit for only one Test. But he showed glimpses of the brilliant form he was capable of and it was very much a case of what might have been.

Already he was becoming a firm favourite

They appointed him skipper in his last year and he tried to instill some of the fifteen-man Rugby that he encouraged Cardiff to play in the late seventies.

The golden era of Welsh Rugby was just beginning, with a draw against France in 1969 denying them the Grand Slam. That summer, Davies toured New Zealand with the national party. It was an unsuccessful visit, but during the tour Davies made the switch from centre to wing, a move that transformed him into one of the finest players of all time, enabling him to delight crowds as his skills were given more room and scope. Clive Rowlands asked him to go out there because of injuries and he was such a success against Australia, that there were thoughts to keep him on the wing permanently. When he returned to London Welsh, there was a glut of top-quality centres – John Dawes, Jim Shanklin and Keith Hughes – so, after much consideration, Davies decided to stay on the wing.

Five tries came his way in the 1971 Grand Slam season for Wales, including the one in the closing minutes against Scotland at Murrayfield; it enabled John Taylor to kick what has been described as 'the greatest conversion since Saint Paul' for Wales's 19-18 victory. His achievements did not stop there that year; he was selected for the Lions with many other members of that disappointing 1969 Welsh party, eager to make up for that failure. Arriving a few weeks into the tour because of exam commitments, Gerald Davies quickly made his mark, bewildering opponents at all levels. He scored ten tries on tour including two in the second Test and one in the third. 'To see Davies in full flight is to see art in motion' was how Willie John McBride described him and there are few who would argue with that or with Willie John.

By now Gerald Davies was an integral part of any Welsh side and played a large part in their accomplishments in the seventies. If there were disappointments for crowds when he did not receive the ball as

The Cardiff crowd begin to cheer as Gerald Davies runs round to score one of his two tries against Ireland in 1971.

with crowds, not least the Twickenham supporters. Although a Welshman, he was their favourite son on Middlesex Sevens days, winning titles with Loughborough Colleges and London Welsh, his sparkling displays brightening up many of their afternoons. And, in 1968, he played in the first of his three 'Varsity matches for Cambridge.

often as they would have liked, he more than made up for that when the ball did come his way. There were many spectacular tries scored by Wales during this period and many were finished off by Gerald Davies. All through his career, he battled neck-and-neck with Gareth Edwards in the try-scoring international stakes. It was fitting that they had both scored twenty each when they retired – Welsh records in international Rugby, although Davies had another three in Tests for the Lions.

The wing was unavailable for the 1974 and 1977 British Lions and most of his later triumphs were with Wales and Cardiff. Just before the Lions visited New Zealand in 1977, Davies proved that he was as good as ever; the try of the season, scored by Phil Bennett for Wales against Scotland at Murrayfield, was made by Davies who countered a Scottish attack and jinked his way out of trouble. Another of his finest displays came in the 1977-78 season in the Schweppes/WRU cup game for Cardiff against Pontypool. Most club games were called off that day and the television cameras gratefully accepted the opportunity to record the thirty-three-year-old wing scor-

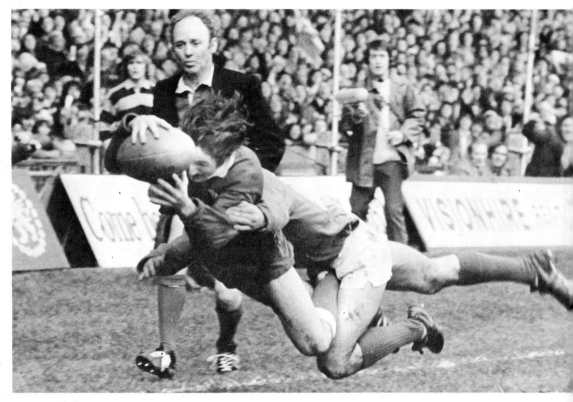

Gerald Davies dives through Wallace McMaster's tackle to score against Ireland in 1975, when Wales triumphed 32-4.

Right Despite being held by two Irish tacklers, Gerald Davies is about to feed Gareth Edwards, who ran through unopposed to score in 1973.

Opposite Gerald Davies shows off his running skills for London Welsh in the Middlesex Sevens, a tournament he also won while playing for Loughborough Colleges.

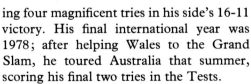

ing four magnificent tries in his side's 16-11 victory. His final international year was 1978; after helping Wales to the Grand Slam, he toured Australia that summer, scoring his final two tries in the Tests.

Davies returned to captain Cardiff for a third season in succession, but he had always insisted that he would give up at the beginning of a season rather than at the end of one–this would give him a chance to see if he could regain his appetite for Rugby. But that season he had not and Gerald Davies decided to call it a day. It was a bitter disappointment for Cardiff, Wales and crowds everywhere, but then supporters had been more than spoilt in watching him play international Rugby for twelve years. To hear talk about Gerald Davies in action and running in tries is always pleasurable and to have seen him play was a great privilege.

Mervyn Davies

The career of the finest post-war British No. 8, Mervyn Davies, ended prematurely when he suffered a brain haemorrhage during a cup-tie near the end of the 1976 season. It was a tragic loss both for Welsh Rugby and the British Lions who were looking for this sensitive Welshman to lead them to victory in the series against New Zealand in 1977. From his international debut, against Scotland in 1969, 'Merv the

Mervyn Davies in his final international appearance when he led Wales to their Grand Slam with victory over France.

Swerve' had become a well-known and well-loved figure on Rugby fields all over the world, quickly recognised as the finest player in his position. Best described temperamentally as the 'strong, silent type', he had a style all of his own—the hunched shoulders with hands on hips, the 'bandit' moustache and the white headband—trademarks which were an integral part of the man who earned respect from colleagues and opponents alike.

He earned that respect by the quality of his footballing skills and the manner in which he approached the game. No. 8 was no longer the man who just leant forward in the scrum with his head between the second rows. Now he played an important

part in directing the push of the eight, as well as controlling that effort. In addition, the link between the No. 8, who was to feed the ball finally out between his legs, and the scrum-half could be of infinite value to a side if that combination worked in harmony. The communication between Mervyn Davies and Gareth Edwards was at its finest on the 1974 Lions' tour of South Africa; they toyed with the ball back and forward and created all sorts of difficulties for the Springbok flankers, who never knew when it was safe to break from the side of the scrum. Mind you, Gareth Edwards was at scrum-half in every one of Davies' thirty-eight internationals for Wales as well as his eight Lions' Tests, so the pair had plenty of experience together. At the tail of the line-out, Davies ruled supreme and his control there was one of the few areas of secure possession the Lions had in New Zealand in 1971. To Colin Meads, the British No. 8 was one of the main reasons for their success in that series.

In the loose, those long, lazy strides seemed to cover miles and Davies was constantly turning up with the vital tackle or linking to keep his side on the attack. Perhaps most importantly, he was a continual source of loose possession for all the teams

Mervyn Davies breaks from a scrum to find his path blocked by England's John Watkins in the 1973 international at Cardiff.

he played for, usually last up at the ruck or maul, uncoiling his six-foot-five frame before preparing to put his head down in a scrum or setting off to support another attack. To cap his career, he was skipper of Wales in his final two seasons, winning the championship both years, the Grand Slam in 1976 and eight of the nine matches in which he was in charge. A few weeks after that Grand Slam triumph, Davies collapsed during the Swansea-Pontypool WRU Cup semi-final.

This beloved Welshman had suffered a brain haemorrhage and almost died. Like all the battles during his career, he won through in the end, but his recovery was slow and he was never to take his place on the Rugby field again. It was a sad end; Davies had seemed destined to cap his magnificent career with one more season leading Wales and then the ultimate honour of skippering

the British Lions. His departure after thirty-eight consecutive appearances (plus eight Tests for the Lions) left a gaping hole in the middle of the Welsh back-row and British Rugby generally. His ball-winning qualities were increasingly appreciated when he was gone as there was no-one to replace 'Merv the Swerve.'

His domination of the world scene had not seemed likely when a gangly, lanky figure took the field at Murrayfield for his first cap in 1969, the same game in which JPR Williams also made his debut for Wales. The newcomer at No. 8 had been born in Swansea in December, 1946, in a Rugby atmosphere—his father had been a Victory international for Wales. Thomas Mervyn Davies first learnt his Rugby at Penlan Comprehensive, later graduating to Swansea College of Education, where he was a Welsh Colleges international at basketball as well as Rugby. After some games for Swansea, Davies, like many others, went east and joined the teaching fraternity and London Welsh.

The distinctive figure of Mervyn Davies on the 1974 Lions' tour of South Africa, where he firmly established himself as one of the all-time greats.

He quickly found his feet and gained international honours after some impressive displays for the first fifteen. At the end of his first international season, Davies travelled with the ill-fated Welsh party that visited New Zealand. Although rather raw, he impressed the All Blacks, though not to the extent he was to do two years later. Many members of that disappointing tour were at the heart of the Lions' determination to win in 1971. And indeed 1971 was a memorable year for the young Welshman; not only did he play a full part in Wales' Grand Slam, but also established himself as the best No. 8 around. It was a position he confirmed over the next few years as he became his country's most important ball-winner. Yet, during the 1974 international season, his form floundered slightly and he found a strong challenge from England's Andy Ripley for the Test spot . . . a suggestion which a year earlier would have been unthinkable.

But Mervyn Davies never gave up anything without a fight; so it was no surprise when he eventually found his best form in South Africa. By the end of the tour, to have imagined the Test fifteen without him would have been unbelievable. Davies left teaching and London Welsh at the end of the 1972 season to become a business representative in his home town of Swansea and was playing for them when selected for the 1974 Lions. His caps while with the London club totalled nineteen, and when his run finished, Davies had added another nineteen with Swansea. It was very fitting that his international career should have been so evenly split between the two clubs to which he gave such dedicated service.

The No. 8 was re-united with his Lions' forward colleagues for the Barbarian's game against the All Blacks at Twickenham in 1974, clinching a draw for his side with a magnificent one-handed try in the closing minutes. Two months later, Davies led Wales for the first time. It was not the easiest of baptisms – his side contained six new caps and they were facing France at the Parc des Princes. But the newcomers and the rest of his charges responded to his quiet, emotive leadership to record an historic 25-10 victory. His only setback as captain came in the 1975 game against Scotland at Murrayfield, but it was still a championship year and Wales went one better in 1976 with their second Grand Slam of the seventies. Davies had suffered a bad leg injury early in that French game, but stayed on as his presence was essential for his side to win. The man who never let London Welsh, Swansea, the Barbarians, Wales and the British Lions down, did not fail at the final hurdle. He stated afterwards that he was looking forward to leading his country to a hat-trick of Grand Slams, but, sadly, that was not to be.

It seemed strange the following season to see someone else wearing a No. 8 Welsh jersey; it had been his, by right, for eight seasons. He had excelled in all departments of forward play as well as in the position of leader. The greatest compliment to this forward is that his game had no weaknesses and there are very few, even among the greats, of whom you can say that. Mervyn Davies was, undoubtedly, a king among kings.

David Duckham

David Duckham was England's most exciting three-quarter since Peter Jackson. Whether in the centre or on the wing, Duckham with the ball in his hands was a sight to thrill crowds everywhere. The blond-haired Englishman's most effective weapon in splitting defences wide open was a prodigious sidestep that seemed to defy the laws of gravity and motion – it took him past the best defenders in international Rugby. Initially looked upon as a centre, Duckham moved to the wing where he emerged as one of the top crowd-pleasers of the early seventies. Of his thirty-six caps for

The partnership that many hoped would be England's saviour – David Duckham passes to his co-centre John Spencer, playing for the Barbarians.

England – a record for a back – fourteen were won in the centre and the other twenty-two on the wing. Ten of those centre appearances were with John Spencer and it looked for a time as if England had at long last found a pair to replace the legendary combination of the fifties, Jeff Butterfield and Phil Davies. But Spencer lost favour with the selectors and, after one game with Chris Wardlow and three with Mike Beese in the centre, the Coventry man moved to the wing. There, when he received the ball, six-foot-one and fourteen-stone Duckham was

able to round or cut through the toughest defence.

And not only was he a brilliant runner, but he appreciated the new co-operation between the wing and the role of the attacking full-back. The man on the end of the three-quarter line had now to be accomplished in defence, with many of the qualities that were better associated with full-back – kicking, catching high balls as well as normal tackling duties. International sides with sprinters on the wing who had little footballing skill could find themselves in all sorts of difficulties. Duckham, as he displayed on numerous occasions on the 1971 Lions' tour, did not have the weak defence that many suspected, coping admirably with varying All Black attacks. It is

44

David Duckham runs round Gloucester full-back Peter Butler to score in a Coventry club game in 1974.

unfortunate that he was not given much chance to shine on the England wing; of his ten tries in thirty-six games, four were scored from the centre and six from the wing. And inside him, England selectors used ten different centre combinations as they tried to find the pairing that would provide Duckham with the ball and space so he could show off the ability that everyone knew he possessed, and convert it into tries.

Perhaps his finest performance was reserved for that classic Barbarians-All Blacks' game in 1973, when Duckham revelled in the atmosphere of adventure that day and responded by producing breath-taking sidesteps on his numerous sorties upfield, his blond hair trailing as were the All Black defenders in his wake. It was a marvellous spectacle, though tinged with sadness that he was not given the opportunity to perform like this for England.

David John Duckham had learnt that sidestep in his final year at the King Edward VIII School, Coventry. The jink came intuitively, making it all the more difficult for defences to counter. He joined Old Coventrians at the age of eighteen in 1964 and three seasons later moved to Coundon Road and the Coventry club. Recognition was swift, Duckham graduating almost immediately to the first team and gaining an

David Duckham, passing to Peter Rossborough in the 1975 game against France, was undoubtedly the most exciting England three-quarter since Peter Jackson.

England trial in his first season. His international debut came the following year in the 1968–69 season, against Ireland, but while he scored a try, England still went down. His centre relationship with John Spencer looked like being a long and fruitful one for England, especially when Duckham scored two marvellous tries to give England victory in the 1969 Calcutta Cup. The newcomer was hailed as the most exciting discovery for many an English season. He toured South Africa that summer with the Barbarians, before resuming his partnership with Spencer the following year. But England could manage just a solitary win in the championship and the duo were to play together only once more in their country's midfield.

Duckham transferred to the wing in 1971 and the second stage of his career began. It was in this position that he was chosen for the Lions' tour to New Zealand that year; his companions on the wing–Gerald Davies, John Bevan and Alastair Biggar–combined with the Englishman to form probably the most talented quartet ever sent abroad in a British party. That visit was one of the highlights of Duckham's career, his form forcing John Bevan out of the side after the first Test. In all, he collected eleven tries, six of them in the game against West Coast/Buller, and gave an outstanding defensive display in the final Test when the draw gave the British Lions the series.

Duckham was unavailable for England's 1972 visit to South Africa, when, after being whitewashed in the championship, the tourists recorded an historic 18-9 victory at Johannesburg in the only Test. But the wing chose the All Blacks for special attention the following season. He led Midland Counties West to triumph over Kirkpatrick's side and then turned in that dazzling display in the Barbarians' game. Furthermore, he travelled to New Zealand that summer, playing an important part in England's remarkable 16-10 Test win in Auckland.

England returned home with high hopes of at last having turned the corner, but it proved to be just another 'one-off'; Duckham, himself, had a bad start to the 1974 international campaign, giving away the penalty in the last minute of the Calcutta Cup game at Murrayfield which enabled Andy Irvine to kick the goal for the Scots' 16-14 victory. England's selectorial policy

was not helping either; in Duckham's final twelve international appearances, there were no less than eight different pairs of centres tried; hardly conducive to finding any sort of continuity or rhythm. Duckham was often left isolated on the wing.

Towards the end of his career, the Coventry wing suffered frequently from injury and seemed to have difficulty finding the sparkle that made him such a major crowd-puller; the expectancy of the exciting, the unorthodox, the out of the ordinary was no longer there. But it was not easy being out on the wing during one of England's most disastrous runs on the international field – only eleven wins in thirty-six appearances and only six in his final twenty-five games. Yet, albeit for too short a time, David Duckham gave English spectators hope. Hope that the golden eras could be recovered and hope that the genius of runners like Butterfield and Jackson could still be found in the modern player, for Duckham had that genius, enthralling crowds everywhere when he was given a chance to do so.

Gareth Edwards

The British Rugby personality of the seventies was Gareth Edwards. 'An explosion just waiting to happen' was how his fly-half partner Barry John once described him and this restless bundle of energy proved himself to be one of the finest players ever seen in the scrum-half position; there are many to support the claim that he was the greatest ever. To watch him continually fulfilling his enormous potential on the international field, despite growing pressure and close marking, was a unique privilege for all who came to see him.

His final international season, 1977-78, was his twelfth; yet he had never been in finer form, using the judgement of all those years to maximise the effect of all his skills. All the qualities that were required for the world's number one spot were in evidence. His tactical kicking, especially up the line, destroyed England at Twickenham, where he led Wales out for his fiftieth consecutive cap. His power and strength led to another try in the home win over the Scots—it was Edwards' twentieth and final try for Wales. His control and steadying power helped keep his side just ahead of Ireland in Dublin to record the third Triple Crown in a row for the Principality. Now only the French at Cardiff stood between their second Grand Slam in three years. Edwards' play that season had been geared to bringing the other players more into the action, as if pointing out that they were soon going to be playing without him. But with his team seven points down, the 'Master' decided to take control. His influence, like many times before, proved decisive. The Welsh machine clicked into action and turned round 13-7 in front, a Gareth Edwards' dropped goal making up three of the points. It is no exaggeration to say that almost everyone present that day could sense the scrum-half's decision to take charge.

Gareth Owen Edwards, even in terms of bare statistics, was a Rugby phenomenon. Fifty-three consecutive caps—never missing a game from the match against France in 1967 to that Grand Slam clash against France in 1978; Wales were only beaten once in the Five Nations Championship in Cardiff during his reign, and that was in 1968; he never lost an international to a British side at the Arms Park; he was made the youngest captain of his country in 1968, aged just twenty; twenty was also the number of tries he scored for his country, a record he jointly holds with contemporary Gerald Davies.

Although Edwards was very much a player of the modern game, his ability was such that he would have succeeded in any era and probably in a number of other sports. Immensely strong, with a low centre of gravity, he was able to barge through any tackle that did not contain a hundred per cent conviction and more than a few that did. His line and tactical kicking, by the end of his career, was of a standard attained by few before—it was purposeful, precise and usually heartbreaking for the opposition. On top of that, Edwards often took over the goal-kicking role for his country and, if not quite as convincing as his kicking out of hand, it was still good enough to save Wales on more than one occasion.

One can judge his determination to succeed by the fact that his passing was one of his weaker aspects of his game when he started. To those youngsters weaned on the never-ending flight of his passes to Barry John and Phil Bennett, the criticism must seem sacrilege. That it may be, but it was fact. Those long, accurate, spiralling passes were the products of many hours of practice.

The only skill that did not fall to him on the Rugby field was that of skipper. He was given the post on more than one occasion by Wales, but he was never convincing in the role. It was not that he could not sum up situations instinctively or was tactically inept; too much of his own game relied on these qualities for there to be a doubt about his ability in these fields. Perhaps he was too tense, too worked up and too involved before games; successful captains have to be different things to different players and often need to stand apart.

Mind you, none of Gareth Edwards' captains had any trouble motivating the Welsh scrum-half. He always gave his all, irrespective of the side and irrespective of age. This competitiveness was a quality that helped him stand out as a schoolboy player.

Born in a small village called Gwaun-cae-Gurwen in South Wales in 1947, Edwards' sporting allegiances were split between soccer and Rugby in his early days; at one stage being offered professional terms by Swansea Town while at Pontardawe school. Luckily for Rugby, the games master, Bill Samuel, wanted to see his prodigy at Millfield, the Somerset school where special attention was given to sporting prowess. Samuel was a very strong influence on the youngster. The physical education master knew the potential of this schoolboy and the need to keep the cheeky

Gareth Edwards passes out in the only game against England in which he was on the losing side in twelve seasons of international Rugby.

Gareth Edwards scores his final try for Wales, his twentieth, in the 1978 game against Scotland.

Gareth Edwards, in the colours of the Rugby Union Writers Club, was a dominating force in the Welsh side for 13 seasons and 53 internationals.

comer was studying at the Cardiff College of Education and playing his club Rugby for Cardiff, where he was to stay all his career. Although Wales lost that day, the scrum-half performed well and might have been hailed the discovery of the season had not another newcomer—an eighteen-year-old full-back—stolen the show in the following and final game of the season, against England at Cardiff. It was the debut to end all debuts; a try, nineteen points in all and Keith Jarrett had helped Wales to a 34-21 victory.

In the following season Edwards teamed up with Barry John in the national side and a partnership was born that lives in Welsh legend; it opened with 'Just throw the ball and I'll catch it.' It was a combination that matured slowly, blossoming in New Zealand in 1971. Both admit that they rarely discussed tactics and many of their moves were spontaneous, yet there was a special relationship and communication between the two, that Edwards never quite achieved with Phil Bennett. It was a time Edwards remembers fondly: 'Because we were younger and at an impressionable age, all our successes seemed that bit special.' Edwards' strength meant that he was able to protect 'King John' and make sure that the fly-half did not suffer at the hands of robust flankers, not if he could help it anyway.

The pair first appeared together against the All Blacks in 1967 and eventually played together 23 times for Wales and five times for the Lions. One of those Lions' Tests was in South Africa in 1968, but both suffered injuries during the tour and were unable to contribute as they would have wished. Before that tour, Edwards had been made captain of Wales for the game against Scotland, but was replaced by John Dawes before the end of the season. Wales won the championship in 1969 and set off for a two-test series in New Zealand full of optimism. But the itinerary was wrong and too hard, there was too little time for preparation, the tourists' form and confidence suffered

lad from floating away on his own wave of success. There was no chance of that when Bill Samuel was around; he helped Edwards to set himself new standards and not to remain satisfied with what he was already achieving. And Edwards earned a place at Millfield, where special concentration could be given to his sport. As well as playing for the Welsh Secondary Schools Rugby side, Gareth Edwards attained the 'honour' of representing England against Wales in the British Schools Athletics Championships after he had captured the English title in the 200-yards low hurdles. Two opponents in those British Championships were JJ Williams and Allan Martin; the three were to share many triumphs, but Edwards was labelled, jokingly, a 'traitor' that day.

Within a few months of leaving school, Gareth Edwards took the field as scrum-half for Wales in Paris on April Fools' Day in 1967, partnering the Welsh captain, fly-half David Watkins. At the time the new-

badly and they lost the Tests heavily. They left New Zealand with their reputations as world-class players in tatters; but the seeds had been sown for the Welsh determination to provide the nucleus of the Lions' side two years later.

Before that Lions' tour, Edwards regained the captaincy of Wales for the game against the visiting Springboks and he saved his side with a dramatic last-minute dive to score in the corner and level the points. But Wales's Triple Crown hopes crumbled 14-0 in Dublin and the captaincy again reverted to John Dawes, who led his side to the Grand Slam in 1971 and the Lions to victory the same year. That 1970 season had given a rare chance to one of Edwards' long-serving understudies. The replacement was 'Chico' Hopkins, who came on early in the second-half of the game against England at Twickenham, with Edwards injured and Wales trailing 13-3. Not the ideal time for someone who had been waiting in the wings for a long time to make his debut. But Hopkins took the opportunity to write his name in the record books as tries from himself and JPR Williams and a Barry John dropped goal led to an exciting 17-13 win.

Being understudy to Edwards can never have been easy as he notched up, with the frustrating air of inevitability, fifty-three consecutive caps. His three main stand-ins – 'Chico' Hopkins, Clive Shell and Brynmor Williams – deserve mention for the patience they showed, especially when they would have walked into most other international sides. At least Hopkins won that cap in 1970 and then Clive Shell came on as a replacement against Australia in 1973, but Brynmor Williams had to wait until Edwards was unavailable for the 1978 tour of Australia before playing his first game for Wales. Unfortunately, after waiting so long, he immediately lost his place to the strong, aggressive Terry Holmes.

The 1971 Lions' tour was a great success for British Rugby and a personal success for Gareth Edwards and Barry John. After

early injury problems, which saw Hopkins again replace him, this time in the first Test against the All Blacks, the Cardiff scrum-half settled down to become an integral part of the Test series victory. After the traumas of the 1969 visit, it was a welcome relief: 'At least Barry and I proved we had some ability and that gave us a lot of pleasure.'

Edwards returned home to score one of the finest individual tries ever seen at the Arms Park; luckily for those absent, the television cameras were there to capture those moments of magic. The try displayed all Edwards' qualities in a few seconds of Rugby genius; it needed strength, judgement, timing, speed, kicking ability, determination and vision. His victims were Scotland. Edwards broke after a scrum in his own '25', powering through the attempts to hold him and he sprinted with the full-back to beat and the cover chasing after him. At just the right moment, he chipped over the defender's head, ran round him and kicked the ball for the in-goal area. Not only had Edwards to reach the ball before Scotland centre Jim Renwick who was chasing hard, but before the ball dribbled over the dead-ball line. Edwards timed his dive to perfection and touched-down before slithering and squelching through the red mud of the Arms Park dog track. He arose, as though blooded in the colours of his country, and went back to halfway to tremendous acclaim.

In 1971, Edwards played behind a Lions' pack that, at best, established parity with their All Black opponents. Three years later in South Africa he was able to perform behind eight forwards whose domination was complete. Edwards commented: 'Their control was so perfect that I could look round, judge the South African defensive plan and then take the ball out at will. It was bliss playing behind them.' In many ways, it was British Rugby's finest hour. It was also the high spot of another of Edwards' special relationships – his almost telepathic communication with the man in the middle of the back-row, Mervyn Davies. They toyed with the Springbok loose forwards, catching them repeatedly offside so that eventually the scrum-half was able to pick up from the scrum unmolested; it was a control unparalleled in Lions' battles against the Southern hemisphere's Rugby giants. Edwards had regained the Welsh captaincy the previous summer for their tour to Canada and retained it for the 1974 International Championship, a season which saw a rare defeat by England, and for the unofficial international against the All Blacks in late 1974. But it was Mervyn Davies who was given the job of leading Wales in the championship later that season.

His final four seasons were a magnificent period for Wales—only two defeats (Scotland in 1975 and France in 1977), three championships, three Triple Crowns and two Grand Slams. It was a unique experience to see so many world-class players at their peak—JPR, Gerald, 'Benny', Mervyn and, of course, Gareth, superbly supported by JJ, Steve Fenwick and Ray Gravell in the backs and the infamous 'Pontypool Front-Row' of Graham Price, Bobby Windsor and Charlie Faulkner plus Allan Martin, Geoff Wheel, Derek Quinnell and Terry Cobner in the pack. All these players, and one or two more, rightly have their place assured in Welsh Rugby history.

And all, seemingly, revolved around this colossus at scrum-half. It was a bitter blow when he announced that he was unavailable for the 1977 Lions' tour. So to his final season and that last Grand Slam; it was a fitting finale. Even when he declared that he was to retire from the game, this exuberant Welshman continued to break records. His autobiography, *Gareth*, became the biggest-selling Rugby book of all time, appearing at the top of the best-seller list for weeks. He was not only a Welsh personality but also a world personality, showing the extent to which Rugby's popularity had grown through the success of the Lions and the changes in the Laws. Gareth Edwards had a lot to do with the game's new appeal; his influence, personality and style attracted many to Rugby. And the position of the man who would rather stand up to his knees in water fishing for salmon than play Rugby for Wales as a Welsh folk-legend is guaranteed for all time.

Douglas Elliot

Douglas Elliot was the outstanding Scottish forward of the late forties and early fifties, a period when Scotland's international results were disastrous. At times it seemed as if Elliot was taking on the opposition in a lone crusade. William Iain Douglas Elliot, or WID as he was known, was a big man for that era of Rugby—standing just under six foot three and weighing fourteen stone—and was a rugged, hard loose-forward, whose game had few smooth edges. His daily farming duties prepared him physically for the rigours of top-class Rugby. And in this regard, Elliot was very much a big occasion player—the tougher and more important the game, the better he played, always responding to the extra challenges and pressures; qualities which emphasised the level of his ability. But this did lead to accusations and doubts about his commitment in lesser matches. It is an attitude of temperament about which there is much argument; but it is a fact of life that certain players need the big occasion to raise the level of their game and play their best.

Elliot's performances on the international field were such that he was respected by all who played with him and treated with respect by those he played against, especially by fly-halves whose delicate ball skills cut little ice if the steamrolling Elliot got his hands on them.

From his first cap in 1947, Elliot played 29 times for Scotland without being dropped, although he did miss five matches near the end of his career because of a hernia opera-

Douglas Elliott passing out against the 'auld enemy', England. His seven Calcutta Cup matches saw him a victor only twice.

tion. Scotland's fortunes were at a particularly low ebb. His six caps against Ireland ended in six defeats; he was only twice a Calcutta Cup winner in seven outings; and he was a member of the Scottish side that was 'lucky to get nothing' in their 44-0 drubbing by the Springboks at Murrayfield on that terrible day in 1951. Yet Elliot's reputation as one of Britain's finest forwards in this period remained unchallenged; even in the worst team display, the flanker would stand out with his total physical commitment and aggressive play.

Elliot, who was born in 1926, was educated at two of Scotland's most famous Rugby nurseries – St Mary's, Melrose, as well as Edinburgh Academy. Although he had some experience of flanker, his first team involvement consisted of three games – all played on the wing. Anyway, Rugby was not that important at the time as Elliot was required to leave school at 16 so that he could help on the family farm; it was wartime, so Rugby became less important for a couple of years. Still, the manual work on the farm kept him fit and when he joined the

two amalgamated Edinburgh clubs – Academicals and Wanderers – before the end of the war, he very quickly made his mark on the senior scene.

Within three years, Elliot was wearing the Scotland colours for the unofficial international against the 1946 Kiwis. Scotland played well that day, winning handsomely. Another bonus was the emergence of a world-class flanker who was to remain in the side for the next eight years.

As mentioned, it was not a happy time for the national side; then, circumstances combined to deprive Elliot of a trip with the 1950 British Lions who were to visit New Zealand. It would have provided a perfect opportunity for Elliot to display his talents in front of an audience who have always appreciated the physical contest and have not always found it from touring British sides. But it was not to be. These were the days when teams travelled to the Antipodes

53

by ship, not plane, and Elliot could not afford to spend so long away from the farm. His father had died the previous year – ironically and fittingly after his son had scored the first try in a rare Scottish win in Paris – so all those months away could not be spared. Yet Elliot desperately wanted to go and offered to fly out at his own expense and join the party in New Zealand, but that offer was declined. It was a sad loss for both British and All Black Rugby and for Elliot.

When he left the international scene in 1954, Elliot had amassed 29 caps, making him then, and still, the most capped Scottish flanker of all time. His presence was a shred of compensation in a trying time for Scottish Rugby and its supporters; it could have been a lot worse if WID Elliot had not been around.

His role can be compared to that of the traditional Scottish warrior – the Highlander . . . brave, aggressive, oblivious to odds and danger, never knowing when he is beaten and whose pride in himself and his country could never be dampened, no matter how many times he was knocked down or beaten. In the end, he prepared to 'die' for his country – and with twenty-two defeats in twenty-nine outings, Douglas Elliot must have frequently felt that Culloden had nothing on this.

Mike Gibson

Midfield back Mike Gibson dominated the British and world scene for the last half of the sixties and the whole of the seventies. When he retired after playing against Graham Mourie's All Blacks in November, 1978, he had set a world-record of sixty-six international appearances; and that did not include twelve Tests for the British Lions. Yet, within five months of his retirement, he was back in the Irish side, this time on the right wing because of injury problems. And not satisfied with that, he was in the Irish party that defeated Australia in the summer of 1979, playing in both Tests.

Never make the mistake of thinking that Gibson's fine international record ever influenced the issue when the Ireland selectors picked their side. Even at the age of thirty-six his talents were worthy of a showing on an international field. 'The most complete footballer' is a cloak that has been placed on his shoulders many times; yet, in a book of superlatives and of superlative players, his position is unrivalled. Very few would have hesitation in naming Cameron Michael Henderson Gibson as centre, or even fly-half, in a 'greatest-ever' team.

And what were the qualities that created a legend long before the subject of the adulation had hung up his boots? Vision, the ability to sum up game situations instinctively, unorthodoxy and improvisation were all part of his make-up. 'A red admiral among cabbage whites' was how All Black scrum-half Chris Laidlaw described the player who, he thought, had 'the problem of being too versatile.' On the attack, his lightning pace would guide him through the narrowest of gaps; he was one of the quickest international footballers of his time and his dedication to fitness and training enabled him to maintain his pace throughout his career and was obviously one of the reasons that he was able to keep his Ireland place. And once he had made his move to the centre, his timing and passing helped create space and opportunities for his colleagues.

For such a fluent, running footballer, his defence was remarkably solid and his tackles earned the reputation of being 'thorough' – there was criticism that he would lay off tackles, shadowing the player to try and divert some other danger. Perhaps he was the victim of his own vision; what may have been obvious to him may not have always been obvious to others. Ignorance is bliss, even to the intelligent Rugby supporter.

In his fly-half days, he proved himself a good tactical kicker and a good goal-kicker; a skill which was needed more than once to

save Ireland. Another hallmark of his class was the way he always seemed to have time to spare – even in internationals – and it is the quality which regularly singles out the sporting genius from mere mortals. Marking Gibson must have been one of Rugby's major headaches; his talents meant that there was an unlimited variety of combina-

Above *Mike Gibson in action on his fifth Lions' tour – New Zealand in 1977. This total has only been equalled by his Irish colleague, Willie John McBride.*

Right *With all that defence, there seems that there is no way that Mike Gibson can score . . . but he did, against Wales at the Arms Park in 1973.*

tions of skills that could be produced in any situation. And while he stood out in any company, it was in the best company that he flourished and blossomed; for many, his performances on the 1971 Lions' tour were the pinnacle of his career. He was a crucial part of what was the most talented back-line ever to represent British Rugby.

His behaviour on and off the field was impeccable, ever the perfect gentleman. Quiet, reserved, dedicated, Gibson was one of the game's great thinkers, perhaps too introverted to ever be totally effective as a captain, though there was no doubting his Rugby brain. On the park, there were no 'hospital passes' from Mike Gibson; he would ride the tackle rather than feed a team-mate in a worse position than himself.

In his early days, there was no gradual promotion for the fresh-faced fly-half who came to prominence in the 1963 'Varsity match. Within two months of his first Blue, he was in the Ireland side and, that Easter, toured with the Barbarians. Brought up in a sport-dominated household, Mike Gibson played scrum-half at preparatory school before graduating to Campbell College, Belfast and the fly-half berth, where he spent two years in the first fifteen.

In the autumn of 1963, he went up to Queen's College, Cambridge, to study law. Gibson excelled in that 1963 'Varsity match, scoring a try in the Light Blues' 19-11 victory. It was the first of three Blues, with the Ulsterman captaining the side in 1965, his final year there.

By the time the 1966 Lions' tour came round, Gibson had played thirteen times for Ireland at fly-half and it was in that position that he was chosen to go to New Zealand. His final law examinations meant that he missed the Australian section of the tour, but, after a slow start, his attacking qualities emerged to the delight of the New Zealand public and he made the Test side in the centre, outside David Watkins. Although the forwards were outplayed in the series, the tour proved a tremendous

experience for Gibson; he was to revisit New Zealand three more times, with the Lions in 1971 and 1977, and Ireland in 1976.

Gibson made up for missing the Australian part of the trip by touring there with Ireland the following year; in a historic victory, the Irish celebrated the first win by a home country in an international in the southern hemisphere. There was travelling again the next summer when the Lions went to South Africa. He played at fly-half in all four Tests, coming on as a replacement for Barry John in the first Test; his scrum-half partners in the series were Gareth Edwards, Roger Young and Gordon Connell. Gibson, like Richard Sharp six years previously, had gained a worldwide reputation for his running skills and he was very much a marked man. But even allowing for his close marking by the Springboks, his attacking talents did not flourish as many would have expected; as ever he was being judged by his own very high standards.

Unbeknown to anyone, his career as Ireland's fly-half was finished. He fractured a cheek-bone just before the start of the 1969 international season and the selectors were forced to introduce young Barry McGann for the game against France. Ireland won well and the newcomer retained his place with Gibson in the centre for the next game.

It is worth noting that 1969 was also the year in which Gerald Davies made his move from the centre to wing; All Black Rugby was to feel the full effect of both these moves a couple of years later. Some said it was the ideal time for Gibson's move to centre, because even the most brilliant player's tricks of the trade can, to some extent, be countered by opposition who know his game after five years as an international fly-half. The phrase 'a change is as good as a rest' must have been inspired by Mike Gibson's move to centre. Gibson's own views on the switch are revealing: 'At fly-half there is involvement, attracting attention from both the opposition fly-half and back-row, and in the centre is the freedom to express oneself.

If anyone had a licence to run, it must be in the midfield, and I have enjoyed myself immensely at all levels when playing in the centre, especially with a fly-half who sets up the moves. In the centre you have the thrill of supporting a move and being able to stay close to the ball.' And even though Gibson was again chosen as fly-half with Barry John on the 1971 Lions' tour, there was little doubt that the Irishman was going to play in the centre in the Tests. The midfield of John, Gibson and skipper John Dawes was a trio of class and vision; Barry John enjoyed playing with Gibson: 'I always felt I was passing the ball to another fly-half. In fact, he often seemed to be an extension of myself.'

For Gibson, too, it was a rewarding experience: 'It was enriching to play in a side that had so much ability. The three midfield men were all of one mind and, when Barry had the ball, I tried to think in terms of something seemingly impossible or unorthodox and then got into position.' It was a team of many talents and all played their part in the success, none more so than Gibson, whom Colin Meads rated, along with Mervyn Davies, as the reason for the Lions' victory in the Test series.

Even though he was to tour twice more with the Lions, Gibson had played his last Test for them. He was unavailable for the 1974 tour, but flew out as a replacement when Alan Old was injured. By then the Test side was settled and giving the Springboks a hammering – there was no reason to change the winning pattern. And in 1977, when his experience was badly needed in the backs, he suffered injury after injury and was never able to sustain a bid for the Test spot. It was a blow, too, to the New Zealand Rugby public who revered this footballer, especially as he had been in such good form with Ireland in New Zealand in 1976. Always a shining light in the Irish side, Gibson had to wait until 1974 for success in the International Championship. The men in green won the title on the day they were

not playing when their two rivals, Wales and France, were both defeated away from home by England and Scotland respectively. It had not only been a long wait for Gibson, but also for Willie John McBride; the pair had shared many disappointments and triumphs for the Lions and for Ireland.

In the 1978 international season, Gibson passed the world record of caps, set by Willie John, when he played in his sixty-fourth game. By now, he was playing on the wing for Ireland, although he was in the centre for his 'final' international – versus the eighth All Blacks; the Irish were unlucky to lose to a last-minute Andy Dalton try in November 1978. Then the evergreen Mike Gibson announced he was bowing out of Test Rugby.

But, the following summer, with another cap under his belt, he was off to Australia with the national side fifteen years after his first Irish cap. Even approaching thirty-seven, 'Gibbo' was in fine nick, with his

Mike Gibson returned to Cambridge University to play in their centenary game against the Barbarians in 1972.

influence on the younger players proving vitally important to Ireland's future hopes. And he played a major part in their magnificent victories in both Tests against the Wallabies. It is pleasing that even in the late seventies Rugby supporters had the opportunity of seeing Gibson in full flight; his type are few and very far between and British Rugby could wait a long, long time before we see his like in the midfield again.

Sid Going

New Zealand scrum-half Sid Going became the greatest individual match-winner in international Rugby since the departure of another All Black, Don Clarke. 'One of our greatest players and one of our poorer scrum-halves' is a description given to him by one of his countrymen. It sums his talents up perfectly. The ability to win matches at the highest level consistently over a length of time is very rare, but Going's determination enabled him to snatch victory for New Zealand in many games, even though opposition teams knew him to be the danger man.

The Lions in New Zealand in 1971 discovered his strength in the second Test when he helped the All Blacks level the series. 'Stop Going' was the order for the next international; it worked because New Zealand then seemed only to play as well as Going did, and their success or failure hinged on his performance. Yet six years later this balding genius was at the centre of the 16-12 triumph over the same opposition, scoring a typically brilliant individual try. But 'typically individual' was the key to 'Super Sid'—so he was closely watched and marked in the second Test in 1977. Again the All Blacks' effectiveness was vastly reduced and the Lions levelled the series.

Sid Going in his final appearance at Twickenham— playing for the All Blacks in their 1974 game against the Barbarians.

There was no comeback for Sid Going this time; he had played the last of his twenty-nine appearances for his country, a record for an All Black scrum-half, and had scored ten tries for New Zealand.

There was no denying the power and determination of this tenacious player, who was totally suited to All Black forward control. He linked expertly with the back-row, forming an especially productive partnership with Ian Kirkpatrick with whom he played many times for the All Blacks. And Going breaking round the side of a scrum or ruck was a very difficult man to stop.

Sid Going kicks ahead in an All Blacks' trial, watched by a young Alan Sutherland and an even younger-looking Ian Kirkpatrick.

His five feet, seven-and-a-half inches and twelve-and-a-half-stone frame had a low centre of gravity and, coupled with an electric pace and powerful hand-off, he was able to break through many tackles. His kicking, especially into the box, was usually inch-perfect and not too comfortable for the player underneath who was waiting for the ball and a two hundred per cent tackle from Sid Going. But his skills were not conducive

Sid Going prepares to hand off Roger Uttley's tackle in the All Blacks-Barbarians' game at Twickenham in 1974.

to running Rugby among the backs. His passing was not his strongest asset, although not as bad as many have made out. All his faults were highlighted and aggravated by his incommunicative attitude and blatant refusal to accept even constructive criticism when offered. Going is a Mormon by faith, dedicated to the church and a very serious-minded person. His religious beliefs would not allow him to play or train on Sundays. There was little humour in his make-up and his philosophy that attack is the best form of defence was an attitude he carried off the field in his dealings with people. He was far too introverted to be a tour captain and his appointment as vice-captain for Kirkpatrick's 1972-73 tour was a mistake; he provided little moral support for his skipper on

the visit, contenting himself with trying to prove that black is white and red is black as far as New Zealand and Welsh Rugby is concerned. It is unfortunate that his surly disposition diverted attention away from his Rugby, which was generally magnificent. Seldom has an international player won so many games almost on his own.

After impressing at Church College School and then North Auckland, Sidney Milton Going's bid for the coveted All Black jersey was halted in 1963 when as a 19-year-old he went to Alberta, Canada, on his two-year missionary work for the Mormon Church. He returned to play against Michael Campbell-Lamerton's Lions for North Auckland and for the New Zealand Maoris.

Although both games were lost, the scrum-half was in top form, scoring a forty-yard try in the Maoris' match. But as far as the All Blacks were concerned, Chris

Laidlaw was the choice for the scrum-half position. Going was pushing him all the way, however, and went as number two to Laidlaw on the All Blacks' visit to Britain and France in 1967. It was only Laidlaw's tactical awareness that kept him in the international side, but he still lost his place to Going for the French Test. It was also Ian Kirkpatrick's debut that day and the newcomers both scored tries in the New Zealand win. Freddie Allen, the coach, had brought Going into the team to unsettle the French, which he did successfully, but the player the coach still wanted at scrum-half to develop his team was Chris Laidlaw. It was not until the 1971 series against the British Lions that Sid Going emerged from Laidlaw's shadow. (Not that Going did not seize any opportunites that came his way. When Carrère's French side visited in 1968, Laidlaw broke a finger before the third Test and Going was in. The replacement was the hero of the day, scoring two tries and narrowly missing a couple more. There is little doubt that New Zealand had a reserve scrum-half who would have walked into any other national team.)

Going toured South Africa in 1970 and played in the first and fourth Tests, but on both occasions still as Laidlaw's understudy. Laidlaw was concussed during the first Test and Going came on to inspire the All Blacks to recover from a twelve-points deficit to 12-9 before the Springboks scored an interception try to settle the outcome. And it was only Laidlaw's appendix operation after the third international that allowed Going into the team for the final match, which the All Blacks lost 17-20. But with Laidlaw opting out of international matches, Sid Going established himself as number one scrum-half, proving a thorn in the side of British Rugby throughout the seventies. He was the outstanding All Black during the 1971 series against the Lions, being the subject of those special 'Stop Going' tactics. Going took this close attention as a compliment to his skills.

As vice-captain on the 1972-73 tour of Britain and France, his Rugby took second place to his criticism of referees who penalised his put-ins, his fiery temper which put him at the centre of many outbreaks of violence (the worst incident was when his punch put East Glamorgan scrum-half Gareth Evans in hospital–'I thought I showed considerable patience before retaliating,' Going said), and his gruff behaviour to all and sundry outside the confines of the tour party. Even allowing for all these distractions, he was again New Zealand's outstanding player, scoring an interception try to seal the game against Scotland and robbing John Moloney, his Irish opposite number, to score another great try in the international at Lansdowne Road.

Going returned to Ireland at the end of 1974 as part of the home country's centenary celebrations, having been left out of the All Blacks side that summer. The scrum-half seemed much happier and relaxed, obviously delighted that his brother Ken had received All Black recognition at last. (These two, with another brother, Brian, had given tremendous service to North Auckland and Maori Rugby. They linked intuitively on the field and their 'special move' brought them many tries. It took a magnificent tackle from JPR Williams in 1971, which stopped Sid Going dead in his tracks a yard from the line, to prevent North Auckland recording a historic victory over the Lions.)

Going returned to South Africa with the All Blacks in 1976. Problems with goal-kicking meant that the scrum-half took over this role, with limited success in the Test matches. Had the New Zealand side had a reliable goal-kicker then victory could have been theirs in the series. When the Lions visited New Zealand a year later, they found the 'old enemy' still there at scrum-half, and still the danger man. It was a point he demonstrated forcibly in the first Test, scoring an individual try that swung the game. Although he was very closely watched in the next international, it was something of a shock when he was left out for the third game. Coach Jack Gleeson wanted fifteen-man Rugby and Sid Going did not fit into his plans.

He may have neglected his backs and it was probably time for a change anyway, but he, along with Ian Kirkpatrick, had been his country's dominant force and personality for a decade. As an individual match-winner, Sid Going had no peer in recent times; the greatest compliment for him is the relief felt by Rugby sides all over the world, especially British teams, when they saw an All Black fifteen that did not contain the name SM Going at scrum-half.

Ken Gray

The New Zealand prop Ken Gray was widely recognised as the best in his position during the sixties. Like Fran Cotton after him, Gray had the rare ability to play on both sides of the scrum with equal success. He packed down at tight-head when his captain, Wilson Whineray, was the other prop, but moved over to loose-head when Whineray retired. On both sides, he was acknowledged as the best in the world.

Exceptionally strong, especially for a man with a long back, his scrummaging power was only one of his attributes; his height – six foot two inches – made him invaluable in the line-out and by the end of his career he dominated the number two jumping position. And while he excelled in the set pieces, Gray was also a talented footballer in the loose – his hands were good and he was a difficult man to bring down when he set off on one of those forward charges which were so typical of All Black forward play in the middle sixties. All this considerable natural ability was harnessed by a quiet, reflective temperament and total dedication. Few props managed to get the better of Gray

Not only was Gray a formidable scrummager, he was also a valuable front-of-the-line jumper as he demonstrates here.

during his international career and most were content just to survive.

This intelligent New Zealander was fortunate in belonging to one of the finest forward units ever to grace a Rugby field – the All Blacks' pack of the mid-sixties. They steamrollered over all that stood in their way – metaphorically, and as some opponents will claim, literally. Unbeaten at international level on Whineray's 1963-64 British tour, they defeated the Springboks 3-1 in 1965 and trampled British Rugby underfoot when the Lions sank 4-0 in 1966. Then it was back to Britain, where the All Blacks were denied the Grand Slam when the Ireland match was cancelled because of the outbreak of foot-and-mouth disease. Ken Gray was an integral part of this golden era – he was only on the losing side twice in his twenty-four Test appearances, and was always a winner in his last thirteen internationals.

Born in 1938, Kenneth Francis Gray had played provincial Rugby for Wellington at lock, his farmer's duties preparing him thoroughly for the rigours of New Zealand forward play, but by 1963 he was in the front-row as a prop and helped Wellington to win the Ranfurly Shield. The selectors expected much of the newcomer and he did not disappoint them when selected for the 1963-64 tour to Britain and France. Making his debut in the Irish Test, which New Zealand won 6-5, he retained his international place for the tour, scoring a try in the victory over France. (Gray was to score three more tries for the All Blacks; one of them in Whineray's final match and one in his own penultimate appearance – the first Test against Wales in 1969, when the European hopefuls were crushed 19-0). Gray had proved one of the outstanding successes of Whineray's tour and had established himself as New Zealand's first-choice prop, a position he was to maintain until his retirement from Rugby.

Gray had been occupying the tight-head spot, but moved over to become the loose-head prop when Whineray was unavailable for the 1964 series against the Wallabies. It was back again to tight-head when Whineray reappeared for the 1965 Springbok series, and by now, Gray had done battle with all the major Rugby countries and his reputation made him a feared opponent. That reputation was further enhanced with his displays against Campbell-Lamerton's Lions and he seemed an automatic choice for Lochore's tour of Britain in 1967, but a month before the trials, Gray had a cartilage removed; that would have been the end of a lesser man's chances. But the selectors never under-estimated his value to the side

Ken Gray is well protected by the rest of his forwards in the 1965 series between the All Blacks and the Springboks.

and a place was kept open for him as he strove to attain fitness. Gray had never let them down and he was not going to spoil that record now; when the sixth New Zealanders reached Britain, Gray was among their number.

The British props and the Rugby public soon realised why every effort had been made to include this Wellington farmer. Even when he injured a hand on tour, he was pressed into service before it was properly healed; it was a mark of the esteem in which he was held by his own party . . . there can have been no finer tribute to this New Zealand prop.

After the two-test victory over Wales in 1969, Gray's influence was looked upon as a vital factor in the All Blacks' attempt to defeat the Springboks in South Africa in 1970. But he withdrew from consideration on moral grounds; Gray felt that he could not tour a country with an apartheid policy. Some of his team-mates felt that he should have gone and seen for himself, at first-hand, the way of life in South Africa and judged for himself. His unavailability did not become known until after the party was announced and was a bitter blow to New Zealand's chances. Many go further and state that the All Blacks would have won if Gray had been a member of the tourists; his loss at the line-out being just as crucial as his loss in the scrum. Colin Meads thinks that with a little persuasion the prop would have gone to South Africa.

Still, most conceded that it was Gray's choice and his decision was to be respected. His contribution to the success of New Zealand's Rugby during his career is almost immeasurable; the forwards certainly lost their way without him. His twenty-four caps make him the most-capped All Blacks' prop behind Wilson Whineray and he has the satisfaction of knowing that during his playing days there was no-one better.

Piet Greyling

One of South Africa's finest loose forwards and a member of a very effective back-row trio which also included Jan Ellis and Tommy Bedford, Piet Greyling excelled both as a creator and a destroyer, a rarity for a top-class flanker who normally fits into only one of those roles. His impact on the international scene was immediate; his six-foot–two–inch, nearly fourteen–stone frame was trained to perfection and his stamina seemed endless. This fitness and his speed around the park enabled him to play a full part in any game in which he took part. One of his strengths was in initiating new attacks and providing support to keep movements flowing and alive. And this tireless flanker constantly turned in defence with a crushing tackle or to secure possession for South Africa.

Greyling was an intelligent player who spent a lot of time thinking about his and his country's role and style of Rugby. Although a tremendous defender, Greyling was basically a constructive player; this, plus an amazing level of consistency at the highest level, made this forward one of the best of the world in the late sixties and early seventies. Many of his international appearances were alongside Jan Ellis and Tommy Bedford; this was one of the quickest back-row units of all time. Opposing half-backs could never expect a peaceful afternoon and any mistake would be instantly capitalised on by this hounding trio.

It was a period when South African Rugby was beginning to feel the full effect of opponents to their govenment's apartheid policy; these outside pressures were eventually felt by the players themselves. This was especially noticeable on the 1969-70 Springbok tour of Britain; Greyling, himself, was in outstanding form, but the general performance of the Springbok forwards was well below par . . . the demonstrations obviously affected some of the players who were distracted from their concentration on Rugby matters.

Pieter Johannesburg Frederick Greyling was born in Rhodesia in 1942, but was educated at the Central High School at Bloemfontein. He made his international debut in 1967. France were the opponents and they, like the South African crowds, were made to sit up and take notice of the performances of this newcomer. Greyling played with total commitment and confidence and he emerged as one of the outstanding forwards in the Test series, which South Africa won. British Rugby had their first opportunity to assess the newcomer when the British Lions toured South Africa

Piet Greyling scores South Africa's only try in their 8-8 draw against Ireland during the Springbok's 1969-70 tour.

in 1968. His promise was evident in the opening Test which the Springboks won 25-20, but he fractured a cheekbone in a provincial game and was replaced by Lourens for the rest of the internationals that year. He was fit again for the two internationals against France that winter: those games plus the four Tests against Australia the following year were all won. Greyling was in particularly fine form against the Wallabies, to whom he was a constant source of annoyance as he was involved in all aspects of play.

The tour to Britain under Dawie de Villiers in 1969-70 was much less successful and none of the four internationals was won, but the flanker scored tries in the matches against England and Ireland and was rated one of the outstanding forwards in the party. He and Jan Ellis became the scourge of British backs who were that yard or two slow in setting up attack situations. However, the games against England and Scotland were lost and only draws were achieved against Wales and Ireland; consequently, this tour is looked upon as a failure, especially in view of the exceptionally high standard set by previous South African sides to have toured Britain.

Greyling's first contact with New Zealand came in 1970 when Brian Lochore brought his All Blacks side to South Africa. The Springbok flanker was in superb form throughout the series, his whole-hearted performances gaining him the respect of the New Zealand forwards. South Africa won the Tests 3-1, yet Greyling's outstanding display came in the second international

65

*Piet Greyling, one-third of a famous Springbok
back-row along with Tommy Bedford and Jan Ellis,
on the attack against France in 1968.*

which the All Blacks won. He was the best
of the loose forwards that day, his dedication
being all the more impressive considering
he was labouring under the handicap of a
strapped ribcage to protect a hairline fracture sustained at Pretoria in the first match.

That win in the first Test had marked the
end of New Zealand's run of seventeen
internationals without defeat; their last
reversal had been by South Africa in 1965.
Greyling recovered for the rest of the games
and his position in world Rugby was reflected when he was invited to England as a
member of the world team that was to celebrate the RFU's centenary in 1971. That
year probably saw Greyling and Ellis at
the peak of their careers. France visited
South Africa for two internationals in 1971
before the Springboks toured Australia for
three Tests. The speed of the two flankers

tory. Of course, some of the blame fell on the captain, but the flanker looked in line to captain the Springboks on their 1973 tour of New Zealand when that tour was cancelled because of political reasons and Greyling led his country on an internal tour instead.

Later that year, at the age of thirty-one, he announced that because of business commitments his days of international Rugby were over. It was a grave loss and South Africa have not yet found any more back-row forwards of the calibre of Greyling and Ellis. Greyling had been a regular in the national side for six years, enjoying singular success apart from that 1969–70 British tour . . . sixteen of his twenty-five international appearances had been on the winning side with four draws. Greyling had earned world-wide respect; one expects the finest in terms of commitment, performance and dedication from South African forwards, standards they have set in the past; Piet Greyling, if anything, set an even higher standard of achievement.

Douglas Hopwood

Douglas Hopwood came to dominate the Springbok No. 8 position in the first half of the sixties. For a large man – six-foot-three and over fourteen-and-a-half stone – Hopwood was extremely mobile and was a joy to watch with the ball in his hands; his repertoire of dummies, sidesteps and jinks belonged to a three-quarter rather than someone who spent a lot of time with his head locked in the middle of the back-row of the scrum. Yet, although his game suited the hard grounds and sunshine of his native land, he did not allow British mud to cover his talents and proved one of the stars on Avril Malan's 1960-61 Springbok tour to Britain. He was devastating as a cover-tackler close to the scrum, preferring to take the ball as well as the man whenever possible. These crunching tackles were

proved too much for both sets of opponents and four games were won and one against France was drawn.

South Africa played only one international in 1972 and that was when John Pullin brought the England side during the summer. It marked Greyling's twenty-fifth game for the Springboks and he was given the honour of leading his country for the only time in his career. Things did not go well for Greyling or South Africa that day and England recorded a historic 18-9 vic-

Douglas Hopwood was one of South Africa's finest running forwards, as he shows here in France during Malan's 1960-61 Springbok tour.

made with total commitment, but were always fair; violence and retaliation were not part of his game.

His footballing skills meant Hopwood was very adaptable to different situations and conditions. If there was an injury in the backs in these days before replacements, it was often Hopwood who would take his place out there, thoroughly enjoying the freedom. He was no fool, either, and would put in deft kicks when the situation required. Whether in the backs or at No. 8, he appreciated the need always to link with his colleagues when possible. If there was no

support around, then Hopwood would chip over the top and follow up rather than allow himself to be swamped by the opposition. A strong mauler, it was in the line-out that he dominated least, although he more than held his own. It is for his running skills that he will be long remembered and he was recognised as the greatest No. 8 in world Rugby during the early sixties. Hopwood served South Africa well, although near the end of his international career he was not treated with the same consideration by Springbok officials.

All sports, not just Rugby, had played a large part in his childhood. Born in 1934, Douglas John Hopwood lived in the suburbs of Cape Town near the coast; soon swimming, skin-diving, fishing and surfing as well as cricket were occupying most of his spare time. Later in his life, golf and snooker were other pastimes he enjoyed.

Hopwood progressed to the international Rugby ranks through the Villagers club and then Western Province. Scotland, making their first-ever visit to South Africa in 1960, were the opposition on his debut, a game which the Springboks won 18-10. The All Blacks visited later that year, but Hopwood did not make the Test team until the third international, when he replaced Nel. The new No. 8 had arrived and was to remain a fairly permanent fixture until his retirement from Rugby after the series in New Zealand in 1965.

Selection inevitably followed for Malan's tour to Britain, where he firmly established his position as world-class. Hopwood made 16 appearances on the tour, scoring seven tries and playing in three of the Tests. His finest performance was in the game against Wales at the Arms Park where his pick-ups and blind-side runs denied the Welsh forwards possession when they were desperate for ball. These charges resulted in Hopwood injuring his back and missing the Ireland international, but the Springboks had gained the 3-0 victory in the Cardiff mud that they had sought.

The No. 8 also excelled in the two other internationals on the tour, scoring the solitary, brilliant try in England's 5-0 defeat and adding another in the win over Scotland at Murrayfield. Hopwood seemed to seize every chance that was offered to him and there can have been fewer more purposeful forwards to have visited the British Isles.

And Hopwood was at the centre of the Springboks' triumphs against Arthur Smith's 1962 Lions when the home side went through the Test series unbeaten. And by the time the selectors came to choose the South African party to tour Ireland and Scotland in 1965, Hopwood was one of the elder statesmen in the team and a strong candidate for captain. His chief rival was Avril Malan, who had led that successful 1960-61 team. Hopwood, himself, had proved an inspired leader of the Western Province, who, against the odds, had won the Currie Cup. Malan's star as captain was on the wane and Hopwood was picked as captain of the first fifteen. The No. 8 was the choice of the selectors, but when the party went to the executive for what was basically rubber-stamping, Hopwood's position as captain was not acceptable.

Apparently, on the 1959 Junior Springboks' tour Hopwood had blotted his copybook when some players had come into confrontation with the manager, Kubos Louw, who was now on the executive. The selectors were asked to nominate a replacement and Avril Malan was their choice; it needs no saying that Hopwood, who was not in the best of health on the tour, gave his all for his captain and for Springbok Rugby. It was a very sad time for the No. 8, denied the ultimate honour of leading his country on the Rugby field. The short tour of five matches was a disaster, four games were lost, including both the Test matches, although Hopwood was in his best form for the match against Scotland.

When the Springboks came home, the search was on for a new captain to lead the side to New Zealand as Malan was unavailable; there was no question of Hopwood being considered, especially as one Kubos Louw was to manage the trip. In the end the post went to the 24-year-old Dawie de Villiers, a scrum-half with only three caps behind him.

Hopwood, who wanted to tour New Zealand before he retired, put in two tremendous performances in the trials and was duly selected. Yet he was not chosen for the team's selection panel on tour even though, at the age of 31, he was one of the party's most experienced players. He suffered a recurrence of that back injury early in the visit and later it was discovered that he had a chip of bone floating about in his right knee. Still, he recovered to play a full part in the last two internationals, inspiring the

Springboks to victory in the third Test. Hopwood was made pack leader for these two internationals, but understandably resented this sop, knowing that it had not been his qualities of leadership which had denied him the right to lead his country. While past his best on this tour, Hopwood's knowledgeable forward play greatly impressed New Zealand observers and he is held in high esteem in that most testing of Rugby countries.

The fourth Test was his twenty-second and final international appearance; it was also Whineray's last match. Hopwood had dominated during his playing career and is remembered throughout the world as one of South Africa's most skilful and knowledgeable forwards.

Andy Irvine

The running skills of Scottish full-back Andy Irvine were a rare compensation in the deteriorating quality of British back play in the seventies. From his precocious debut against Ian Kirkpatrick's All Blacks in 1972, he has endeared himself to crowds all over the world with flair for attack in any situation. While there may be some question marks over the soundness and concentration of his defensive play at full-back, there is no doubt about his talents as one of the finest runners with a Rugby ball in his hands of this or any era.

As a pupil at George Heriot's School, Edinburgh, he was destined to be Scotland's full-back almost by tradition and right. Seven previous Scotland full-backs – Dan Drysdale, Jimmy Kerr, Tommy Kerr, Ian Thomson, Ken Scotland, Colin Blaikie and Ian Smith – all went to Heriot's, so Andy Irvine could have had no finer pedigree. And the last five named plus Irvine have all played for their country since the last war.

Famous names to follow, but Andrew Robertson Irvine exuded class and confidence from his first touch of a Rugby ball and quickly established a reputation as one of the most dangerous attackers of recent times. And playing at full-back gave Irvine the space and opportunity to expose any flaws in opposition defences. While he may be shaky under the towering ball, fly-halves are still very hesitant in putting their boot to the high kick. Sure, Irvine might drop the ball, but then again those fly-halves may just be presenting the full-back with the chance to make one of his match-winning counter-attacks.

Some of his international Rugby has been played on the wing. With JPR Williams in charge at the back on the 1974 Lions' tour, Irvine was to be found outside the centres in the third and fourth Tests, while Bruce Hay has been preferred to Irvine on several occasions as Scotland's full-back. Both these players have sounder defensive techniques than Irvine, but the Heriot's player is so gifted that he could not be left out. Often his errors in defence would be due to seeming lapses in concentration, or more probably, because his mind was already working out how he was going to beat the first player on his run upfield. And he is no slouch either, having won the 100, 200 and 400 metres titles at school. Not for him the refuge of a quick kick to touch!

With his three tries in the 1979 International Championship – a record – he took his total for Scotland to seven, also a new record for an international full-back. And Irvine is a prodigious goal-kicker in addition to his running ability; holding the Scotland record in that department, too, with 147 points in thirty-three appearances (until the end of 1979). The Lions were grateful for his record one hundred and fifty-six points in South Africa and his eighty-seven points, including eleven tries, on the 1977 New Zealand trip. As well as his running and kicking skills, Irvine's confidence on the field is a great boost for his team-mates and he helps them to rise to the big occasion.

Above Andy Irvine, the most-capped Scottish full-back of all time, breaks through against the French at Murrayfield in 1974.

Right Andy Irvine breaks away from Allan Martin during Scotland's home game against Wales in 1977.

Irvine's career has coincided with the development of the formerly negative last line of defence into one of the game's most potent attacking forces. Not so long ago, being selected for full-back was on a par with being put in goal at soccer. But the kicking dispensation law and the desire to make Rugby a more attractive spectator sport has now given the full-back more scope than anyone else on the Rugby field.

Irvine has the ability to exploit this new role to the full.

Even before his international debut, Irvine had played on the wing. When he joined Heriot's FP, the full-back berth belonged to international Colin Blaikie, so the youngster had to bide his time on the wing, where he also played for the Edinburgh district. The current national full-back was Arthur Brown, of Gala, who unfortunately broke his leg playing for the Rest of Scotland Districts against the 1972-73 All Blacks. There were also injuries to other contenders, and so the twenty-one-year-old Edinburgh University student

Andy Irvine stepped up to make his debut. It was a memorable day, the occasion in no way curbing his attacking instincts and the All Blacks struggled to contain this debutant, who also kicked two huge penalty goals. But the result that all Scotland wanted was not to be, Sid Going scoring an interception try in the dying minutes to seal New Zealand's 14-9 win.

The new full-back had set himself high standards, but maintained his form and was selected as number two to JPR Williams on the 1974 Lions' tour of South Africa. By the time of that trip, Irvine had already played in two historic Calcutta Cup matches. In 1973, under the leadership of Ian McLauchlan, Scotland were striving to win their first Triple Crown since 1938, but disappointingly went down at Twickenham at the final

Andy Irvine runs round behind the posts to score one of his seven international tries from full-back. The opposition this time are Wales at Murrayfield in 1977.

hurdle. But that was all forgotten a year later when Irvine kicked a last-minute penalty goal to squeeze out England's challenge, 16-14. Earlier in the game, he had scored his first try for his country and was fittingly chaired off the field.

In the early stages of that 1974 Lions' tour, Irvine was becoming a 'forgotten' man, suffering nightmares in defence. But with help and coaching, he knuckled down to finish as one of the great successes. He replaced Billy Steele on the wing for the final two Tests and finished up with one hundred and fifty-six points, a record. His boyish good looks and his attacking style made him a firm favourite with the crowds, becoming the number one pin-up like Tony O'Reilly nineteen years earlier. That attacking style brought about an affinity with Rugby spectators everywhere, who appreciated his desire to run with the ball.

The following year saw another Triple Crown bid disappear at Twickenham and then came Irvine's first visit to New Zealand when he toured with Scotland. Scotland lost 24-0 in the only Test, played in the most appalling wet conditions. Bruce Hay wore the number 15 jersey that day, with Irvine on the wing, but Hay, who was making his debut, broke his arm and Irvine ended up at full-back.

With JPR Williams unavailable, Andy Irvine was given a chance to establish himself as Britain's leading full-back on the 1977 Lions' tour to New Zealand. After his almost customary shaky start in defence, Irvine progressed to be hailed as the top back and the star of the visit. His running from unorthodox situations took the New Zealand players by surprise and delighted the crowds. He ran in five tries against Colin Meads' side, King Country, and scored a magnificent solo effort from halfway against Combined Canterbury.

The Test series was tight and the All Blacks, knowing his capabilities, rarely kicked near Irvine. Also, the quality of the Lions' back-play did not help create much space for Irvine's intrusions into the three-quarter line.

Towards the end of the seventies, the Scots had the best back-line in the championship, but unfortunately their fine pack of a few years earlier was already breaking up and the forwards were having great difficulty in winning the ball. Irvine could not be kept out of the limelight, however, and scored tries against Wales, Ireland and France in the 1979 International Championship.

It was a special season for him because he led Heriot's to their first Scottish League Championship, after Hawick had won the first five in succession. Heriot's won the title by playing the type and style of Rugby associated with their skipper. His example had not only been followed by his own club, but by full-backs all over the world who used this new freedom to add another dimension to their game at full-back and to Rugby, in general. Andy Irvine had played a major part in that development.

Peter Jackson

Peter Jackson was a world-class wing who ghosted his way through packed defences with bewildering ease. His twenty caps for England were scant reward for the most talented back to represent England since the war. Any and every trick would be used in his efforts to beat opponents and they usually worked; defying logic and the most packed defences, he would weave his magic way through to score tries that are still talked about today. His repertoire was endless – sidesteps, dummies, zig-zagging his way across field, cross-kicks – Jackson was always the danger man and a constant threat, able to make something from nothing and steal the game from under the opposition's noses.

His guile and jinky running led to accusations that he was not the quickest of wings,

Peter Jackson, the best wing three-quarter produced by England since the war and probably their finest of all time.

but it was just that his style belied his turn of speed. Jackson rarely allowed himself to be pushed or tackled into touch, but instead would venture in-field looking for support or a gap through the defence. Once in confrontation with a defender, he would either throw one of his contrived dummies (which would often cause the tackler to botch his tackle or miss him completely) or produce one of his outrageous dummies in which very often he would be seen to be offering the ball to the defender before pulling it back and leaving yet another player floundering in his wake. Another trick was to pretend to kick over the approaching player, who would turn and chase for the ball that was still in Jackson's hand. By the end of his career he had an almost paralysing effect on the opposition, especially the wing who was assigned to mark him. That wing could never relax because Jackson was prepared to attack from anywhere; this made him a great favourite with the crowds, not only in Britain, but in New Zealand and Australia where he was one of the Lions' stars in 1959.

Peter Barrie Jackson was born in Birmingham in 1930 and attended the King Edward's School, Birmingham. There he represented the first fifteen as well as holding the school athletics records for 100, 200 and 880 yards; not bad for a 'slouch' whose pace was later questioned on the field. The first six years after school were spent with the Old Edwardians before he joined Coventry in 1954.

By now, Jackson was on the wing; he had started at fly-half, but his talents were better utilised outside the centres. Jackson claims that it was his selfishness that led to the 'exile' on the wing. Whatever the reason, Coventry, Warwickshire, England and the British Lions had found a rare talent indeed. Surprisingly, the Barbarians cannot be added to that list of honours. Early in his career he had been asked to play, but had called off late. His excuse was that he was injured, but he really wanted to play and by delaying his decision, he could give himself as much chance as possible of being fit; but time ran out, and the Barbarians never asked him again. His absence from their number is probably the most glaring, and certainly the saddest, omission in that club's distinguished role-call. If ever there was one player who epitomised the Barbarians' style of running Rugby, it was Peter Jackson.

England wanted and needed him, though, and Jackson made his international debut against Wales in 1956. It was the beginning of an international career that was to stretch

Peter Jackson in the game that brought him immortality, at least in Rugby circles. The England-Australia clash at Twickenham in 1958.

to 1963, although in that time he only played three full seasons for England—1957, 1959 and 1963. In fact, after his triumphant return from the 1959 Lions' tour, he was only to represent his country on five more occasions.

Of his two most famous tries, fittingly, one was scored for England and one for the British Lions. His try for England was such that he dived over into the 'Twickenham Hall of Fame.' The opponents that day were Australia and the play was robust to say the least. Fly-half Horrocks-Taylor was carried off after twenty-five minutes and Jeff Butterfield, who moved in to partner Dickie Jeeps, was laid out. Still, England battled hard and had seemingly done the impossible when they levelled the scores with a penalty goal almost on full-time.

But the encounter had entered several minutes of injury time when the home crowd went berserk. England won a line-out on the Wallaby '25' and the ball went along the line (including via Peter Robbins who was playing in the centre in those days before replacements) to Peter Jackson. The Australian wing's tackle was half-hearted and Jackson was past him; full-back Terry Cauley knew Jackson's liking for coming inside and thought he had his man covered before Jackson double-shuffled, feinting inside before swerving outside again. The wing, Phelps, who had missed him, re-covered, but his tackle was too late to stop Jackson diving over to score in the corner. Mere words cannot convey the tension and then euphoria that erupted. Suffice to say that it was a try that only he could have scored. It was one of the wing's finest moments; he recalls: 'I can remember it so clearly, and recall how exhausted I felt after evading Terry Cauley and diving over.'

He was nicknamed 'Nikolai' when touring with the Lions the following summer – Jackson had a very pale complexion and a set expression that never changed. This was in total contradiction to his performances on the field and the Australasian crowds loved this world-class entertainer. He scored six-teen tries in the New Zealand part of the tour – one behind his fellow tourist Tony O'Reilly – and two of them were in the Test series. It was a series of frustration for the Lions, who spent a lot of time watching Don Clarke taking his deadly aim. As they entered the final game, they were three Tests down, which gave an utterly unrealistic picture of the balance of power between the sides. That balance had to be corrected, albeit too late, and this the Lions did, scor-ing three magnificent tries to the inevitable two penalties from Don Clarke. Bev Risman, Tony O'Reilly and Peter Jackson were the Lions' scorers, with Jackson again proving that he could score when no-one else would even consider the possibility of a try.

The All Blacks were leading 3-0 when the Lions won a line-out, and Jeeps set his back-line moving. O'Reilly, the blind-side wing, had come into the line outside Risman and sent the defence into disarray, punching his way through the middle before feeding the ball to Ken Scotland. 'Feeding' is used loosely here, the ball was actually flung in Scotland's vague direction. Scotland drew the full-back, Clarke, before giving the ball to Jackson who was thirty-five yards out with three defenders between him and the line. It seemed futile and a cross-kick looked the only way out; that is, to everyone but Peter Jackson. Seconds later, after a com-bination of sidesteps, dummies, changes of pace and juggling of the ball, All Black bodies littered the '25' and Jackson had put the Lions level. As usual, Jackson had hypnotised the defence into letting him through; to many there that day, that seemed the only explanation. It is a try still talked about in New Zealand and, indeed, all over the Rugby world.

Although he played a full part in the last England Championship win (up to 1979) – 1963 – most of Jackson's future successes were with his county Warwickshire, who were to appear in six of the seven county finals up to 1964. They won the title hat-trick starting in 1962 and Peter Jackson led them each time. His final final was his last game in his last season and the wing rates it as the most memorable game he has ever played in. He had been suffering from a spinal disorder which plagued him all that season and which necessitated him giving up the game. After every game that season, Jackson would have to visit his Birmingham doctor, who fortunately was a Rugby enthusiast. Lancashire were the opponents in the final and Jackson knew a mammoth effort would be needed to beat them. His side responded and, thanks to a Jackson try and a late push-over effort, the hat-trick of titles was theirs. It was a proud moment for the England wing in his last appearance; he could not have asked for a happier ending.

Peter Jackson considered himself a better player as his career progressed. He said that his feet used to move considerably faster than his brain, but now that his feet had slowed down, he had produced a better sense of co-ordination and was catching up with himself. That may or may not be true, it doesn't really matter; instead, those who saw him in action should just be grateful for the opportunity of having seen one of the most talented and mesmerising crowd-pullers ever to grace the Rugby field.

Barry John

Welsh fly-half Barry John earned the nickname 'King John' and became Rugby's first superstar after the 1971 series between the Lions and the All Blacks. Few people would have been better equipped to cope with the adulation and success than Barry John, although he does emphasise that these pressures played a large part in his decision to retire at the age of twenty-seven in 1972. This good-looking, easy-going Welshman has many supporters for the claim of the finest Rugby player of all time.

John was a joy to watch, feeding on the long service of Gareth Edwards before ghosting his way through defences or putting in telling, tactical kicks. Somebody once pointed out that it was reassuring to see Barry John leave by the door, and not simply disappear through a wall. His kicking out of hand during the first Test on the 1971 Lions' tour had New Zealand full-back Fergie McCormick arriving just as the ball was dribbling into touch or leaving him with no space to work in; it was a nightmare and tormenting time for the All Black full-back, who was no fool, and he can thank Barry John for ending his international career. The New Zealand selectors were

Barry John, Rugby's first superstar and the outstanding player on the 1971 British Lions' tour of New Zealand.

hasty in dropping McCormick, but the fly-half's kicking that day had been the model of perfection and effectiveness. Also, on that tour he emerged as a world-class goal-kicker, breaking records wherever he went. As a fly-half and link, he brought out the best in one of the most talented Lions' back-lines ever assembled – Gibson, Dawes, Duckham, Gerald Davies and John Williams at full-back. The New Zealand

Barry John, for whom 1971 was a memorable year, as he inspired Wales to the Grand Slam, then the Lions to victory in New Zealand.

crowds were delighted with the British backs' running in the provincial matches and Barry John was hailed as the 'King' among princes; his name will last for ever in that home of Rugby.

Barry John's name will always be spoken in the same breath as Gareth Edwards. There was an immediate chemistry between them, right from the very start when the scrum-half found out that his future fly-half partner was not all that keen on training and practising, especially in the wet: 'Look Gareth, you throw them – I'll catch them. Let's leave it at that and go home.' And basically that is what they did for the next six years. Barry John had a unique style about him, even off the Rugby field; success came naturally and easily to him and the fame never affected his pleasant, warm personality.

The future Welsh fly-half was born in the village of Cefneithen in Carmarthenshire in January, 1945. Living opposite him on the other side of the local park was another international fly-half, who was to coach the 1971 Lions and who was to have a profound effect on John's career, Carwyn James. John's natural ability showed itself in many sports other than Rugby in his schooldays, which were spent at Gwendraeth Grammar School. Barry, along with his three brothers, Del, Alan and Clive, all played for the local team, but bigger things awaited Barry and he was invited to play for Llanelli, where he spent three seasons.

In his final year at Trinity College, Carmarthen, the young fly-half won his first Welsh cap, against the Wallabies in late 1966 replacing David Watkins, who had won eighteen consecutive caps as well as playing in the four Tests for the Lions that summer. His scrum-half in the Australian game was Abertillery's Alan Lewis, who was replaced by Cardiff's Billy Hullin for the next game, against Scotland. Wales lost both these matches and the new fly-half had given the impression that, although he undoubtedly had potential, he was not quite ready for the international scene. David Watkins was recalled, and alongside him for the final two internationals was newcomer Gareth Edwards.

John's bid to regain his place was made easier when Watkins turned professional that summer and John joined Cardiff to link up with Edwards. The pair played at half-back for Wales during the next season, which was a transitional one for the national team. The combination was beginning to click together and both were selected for the 1968 British Lions' tour to South Africa. Unfortunately, both suffered injuries, John's being the more serious as he broke a collarbone during the first Test. Although there were criticisms that he made too many wrong judgements and was sometimes too greedy, the conditions suited his style and he was beginning to fulfil his promise when the

Barry John takes a left-footed drop kick during Wales' Grand Slam season in 1971.

injury came. Still, the Welsh side were becoming a force to be reckoned with and only a draw in Paris denied them a Grand Slam in 1969, although the championship and a Triple Crown made up for the disappointment. The half-backs travelled to New Zealand that summer with the Welsh side, but did little to enhance their reputations with the New Zealand critics in what was generally a disappointing tour. It was a bitter blow but many of that Welsh contingent saw the chance to make amends in the British Lions' tour two years later.

If ever a year belonged to one man then 1971 belonged to Barry John; he could do nothing wrong and his guardian angel must have been in close attendance for those twelve months. Firstly, he played a major part in Wales's first Grand Slam for nineteen years. In light of the tremendous reputation he achieved as a match-winning goal-kicker in New Zealand that summer, it is interesting to note that he was not his country's first-choice at the start of the year. That was not because there was anyone better, just that John's talent in that department had not come to light. With the Triple Crown won, Wales travelled to Paris, where many of their Grand Slam hopes had floundered in the past. Barry John rates that French game as the finest he played in and the try he scored as his best. He had always admired the style and passion with which the French played their Rugby combined with their unorthodox thinking. The fly-half was not all that well-known for his relish of the physical commitment in defence, but he played a full part that day, sustaining a broken nose when preventing Dauga from scoring. John stayed on the field to kick a penalty goal to give his side a 6–5 lead, the other points coming from an Edwards' try after a magnificent interception and run from his own '25' by full-back John Williams. Then John scored a marvellous individual try from a set scrum, tearing the French defence apart to give Wales a 9-5 victory and the Grand Slam. That was normally enough excitement for one year, but in many ways it was just the end of the beginning that year for Barry John.

Many of that Welsh side provided the nucleus of the Lions' party that was skippered by John Dawes; there were scores to be settled after that disastrous 1969 Welsh tour and Edwards and John wanted to show the crowds what they were really capable of. John reached the century of points in only eight games, setting a record for a tourist in New Zealand, and finished the tour with a tally of one hundred and eighty-eight points. But his adulation hinged on much more than just his goal-kicking. His general play was of an exceptionally high standard, providing journalists and commentators with the problem of finding new words to describe his consistently superlative displays. His destruction, almost assassination, of Fergie McCormick in the first Test has already been described and was the key to the opening victory. The second international was lost and Barry John summed up the general feeling before the third game: 'The feeling I had before this match was that everything I had done before in Rugby would have counted for nothing if we did not win this match. It was going to be the most important match I was ever to play in.' The 'Stop Going' operation worked and tries in the opening minutes from Gerald Davies and Barry John gave the Lions the lead they needed to win the game. A draw in the last match meant the Lions had won the series and Barry John was hailed as the finest fly-half to have visited New Zealand's shores. His appeal carried right through the touring party, so much so that when the players started singing the national anthem at post-match banquets, 'King' was substituted for 'Queen' – and it was meant as no disrespect to Her Majesty.

When he returned home, he found the adulation had spread throughout Wales, making it difficult for him and his family to lead a normal life. There was also pressure on him to capitalise on his fame and on Rugby's ever-growing popularity. He retired, many thought prematurely, after three more games for Wales in the 1972 international season. The match against Ireland was cancelled because of the political pressure, yet John still managed to notch up thirty-five points in his three appearances, finishing with four penalty goals against

France. His points tally for his country was ninety, a new record for Wales, although this was soon overtaken by Phil Bennett.

Barry John played twenty-five times for the Principality, but he will never be remembered in mere statistical terms. He had a charisma all of his own, an attraction which went well beyond the bounds of Rugby, based on much more than his footballing ability. 'BJ' was one in a million and we all knew it.

Peter Johnson

The fine career of burly hooker Peter Johnson covered three decades. From his international debut in an Australian jersey, against Ronnie Dawson's British Lions in 1959, until his final appearance, against France in the 1971-72 season, Johnson dominated the middle of his country's front-row and was a respected figure all over the Rugby-playing world. Capped at a very early age for a member of the scrum – only twenty-one – Johnson's first thirty-four caps were consecutive (thirty-seven if you include his three matches against Fiji in 1961) and he led his country on more than one occasion. Johnson formed a fruitful relationship with Wallaby scrum-half Ken Catchpole at club, state and international level; Catchpole's feeding and Johnson's quick striking ensured safe and quality scrum ball for Australia in their matches together. If the hooker went down in the tight-heads, then it was more than likely that he was playing with a different scrum-half.

This guarantee of his own ball would have been enough to secure his place in the Test team, but Peter George Johnson was able to combine his specialist talents with those of a foraging forward in the loose. Those reflexes which were so much part of his trade in striking for the ball in the scrums also served him well around the field, supporting and carrying on attacks by backs and forwards alike. His role in the line-out was

Recognition of Peter Johnson's great services to Australian Rugby came in 1971 when he was selected as a member of the world side that celebrated England's centenary.

geared towards helping the jumper and then protecting the possession gained. And this ancilliary role in international Rugby throughout the sixties earned Peter Johnson the deserved reputation of being a 'forwards' forward'; his colleagues appreciated his unselfish style of play.

Born in 1938, the future Wallaby hooker started his club career with the Eastern Suburbs side, but they did not believe the youngster had any special potential, so he took his talents to Randwick. Randwick viewed Johnson in a more favourable light, considering his five foot eleven inches and fourteen-stone build as ideal for a hooker.

81

Peter Johnson scores the Wallabies first try on their tour of South Africa in 1963, when they upset the form-books by drawing the Test series.

And when Ken Catchpole arrived at the club, his career took on a new impetus.

Although Peter Johnson made his debut against the British Lions of 1959, the hooker had to wait four years before he walked off the field as an international victor. His first victims were England and then later that summer Johnson was a member of the Wallaby party that surprised the Springboks by drawing the series 2-2. The average age of that party was only 22 and twelve tourists were previously uncapped. Yet, they went into the final Test with a 2-1 lead and returned home with the finest record of any Australian side in South Africa. The secret of their success were the forwards, with Johnson being singled out particularly for his quick striking. It had been a long wait for Johnson, who had already captained the Wallabies in the Brisbane Test against the All Blacks in 1962.

Australian international Rugby was on the up. When they beat New Zealand 20-5 in the third Test at Wellington in 1964, John Thornett's side was rightly recognised as a world force. And if any confirmation was needed, Australia's 2-0 victory over the Springboks in 1965 provided it, with Peter Johnson at the centre of not only those Test victories but also New South Wales' historic triumph over the tourists. After playing in the games against Campbell-Lamerton's Lions, Johnson made his first tour to Britain during the 1966-67 season. Thornett's side beat Wales and England, losing to Scotland and Ireland and the tour was one of the high spots of Johnson's career, his association with Ken Catchpole ensuring a good supply of ball for the Wallaby backs, for whom Catchpole and his fly-half partner Phil Hawthorne were outstanding.

Unfortunately, this scrum-half and hooker partnership was abruptly ended in the Australian-New Zealand series of 1968. The scrum-half, with a leg trapped, was vigorously yanked out of a maul by Colin Meads by the other leg and Catchpole's international career was at an end. Johnson took over as captain, leading the Wallabies on their unsuccessful short tour of Ireland and Scotland in 1968. This was the end of his thirty-four consecutive appearances in the yellow jersey. He was unavailable for the 1969 visit to South Africa where the Wallabies were whitewashed.

Johnson returned to play five more times for his country, finishing on the short tour of France, where the series was shared at the end of 1971. So, after thirty-nine games against international board countries (plus those three against Fiji), Johnson called it a day as Australia's most-capped hooker and player, a record he now shares with flanker Greg Davis. It had been a period when the Wallabies reasserted themselves as a world power in international Rugby and Peter Johnson's name will always be associated with the Wallabies' drive to the top.

Ian Kirkpatrick

'Kirkie' as he was known to the whole Rugby world, was a permanent member of New Zealand teams for the decade leading up to 1977. His international career began at No. 8, but he was soon on the side of the scrum, displaying all the highest qualities of his famed predecessors, Nathan and Tremain. Ian Kirkpatrick was a model All Black, playing the game with the strength of dignity that has always been the hallmark of the top Rugby men from that country.

Groomed to lead his country, 'Kirkie' was much more a world-class performer in his own right than the previous skippers, Whineray and Lochore, had been. Yet, his period of leadership is looked upon as one of the least successful in terms of results and the All Black image. It would be a disservice to the player if the bad feeling created on the 1972-73 tour to Britain and France was allowed to overshadow Kirkpatrick's personal achievement as a New Zealand forward.

As captain, Ian Andrew Kirkpatrick set standards of play and behaviour that his team-mates, who to all extent and purpose revered him, did not seem to want to follow. The senior and older players were sadly unaware of their responsibility to Rugby, New Zealand and Kirkpatrick. Eventually, he was replaced as skipper, but not as flanker, as he carried on in an All Black jersey for another three seasons, bowing out after the 1977 series with the Lions. It is very rare for this to happen. Brian Lochore returned in 1971 under Colin Meads, but only because the All Blacks were in dire straits; it was not a happy comeback. That Kirkpatrick was able to play so well and successfully under Andy Leslie (1974-76) and Tane Norton (1977) again highlights the man's unselfish character and dedication to his country's Rugby.

Ian Kirkpatrick was an outstanding athlete at school in Christchurch. Not only did he captain the first fifteen, but was also heavyweight boxing champion, and his athletics specialities were the hurdles and pole vault. This sixteen-stone, six-foot-three, twenty-one-year-old forward attracted the New Zealand selectors as they were choosing the party to tour Britain under Brian Lochore in 1967. As cover for the captain, Kirkpatrick could expect to play only a minor role on the visit; but his considerable talents and physical presence ensured attention and Kirkpatrick forced his way into the Test side for the game against France on the flank at the expense of Kel Tremain. It was a memorable All Black win; the newcomer scored a try and broke his nose!

That injury meant Tremain returned for the next international against Scotland, but the youngster had arrived and was to play in the next thirty-eight consecutive New Zealand internationals—an All Black record—finishing when the Lions returned home in 1977. Despite not being selected for the first international the following year, against Australia, Kirkpatrick came on as replacement for Brian Lochore at No. 8 when the captain retired injured after twenty-five minutes. This made him the first New Zealander to come on as a substitute for twenty-one years, but his achievements that day were far from finished; Ian Kirkpatrick became the first replacement to score three tries in an international and the first All Black to score three tries since Pat Caughey, against Scotland, in 1935. (It was also the game which saw the end of Ken Catchpole's career when he was vigorously pulled out of a ruck by Colin Meads when the scrum-half's leg was trapped.)

With Lochore unavailable for the next two games, 'Kirkie' took his place at No. 8, after which time all his international Rugby was played on the flank.

Kirkpatrick's performances in the series against Wales (1969), South Africa (1970) and the British Lions (1971) all served to confirm his position as an obvious member of any world fifteen (which he was, in fact, when he took part in the RFU's centenary celebrations in 1971). Ian Kirkpatrick was already establishing a reputation as a try-scoring forward. In his career, he scored sixteen times for the All Blacks, easily a record for New Zealand and also a record for any international forward. He notched up a try every year of his international career except 1975 when Scotland were the only opposition. He seems to have treated Scotland kindly, because they are the only international board country which he did not score against, although there were a few Scots in Lions' jerseys when he scored in 1971 and 1977.

Both his tries against the Lions were memorable efforts, and very necessary to his country's success. After defeat in the first Test, the All Blacks just had to win the next one in 1971. They did so in magnificent fashion, with 'Kirkie' scoring one of the outstanding tries in international Rugby. He broke through a maul in his own half, shrugged off JPR Williams' despairing tackle and raced away for the try; mere words do not convey the power, skill and determination which Kirkpatrick showed that day.

His try in the third Test in 1977 came after fifty-four seconds and was a very simple effort indeed; but with six changes in the All Black side, it gave them the start they needed to clinch the game and ultimately the series. It was his final international score, setting a record which will take some beating. Although all countries suffered, Australia was singled out for special punishment—eight tries in eight internationals against the Wallabies. They must have been pleased when his career was over.

The low-point of Ian Kirkpatrick's career was his nine-match international reign as All Black captain. The results were not that bad—the first six games were won, the seventh drawn and the next two lost—but it was a transitional period for All Black Rugby and at times, Kirkpatrick seemed to be fighting a lone battle for his side.

The 1972 series against Australia went well enough; three Tests won, ninety-seven points for, twenty-six against, and sixteen tries scored in the three matches. Kirkpatrick's ability to lead had not been put under pressure and there was plenty of optimism as the party set out for the tour to Britain and France. He was very soon to discover the real pressures of captaincy. The management was weak and his vice-captain, Sid Going, became one of the chief protagonists rather than the skipper's right-hand man. Certainly Kirkpatrick did not crack down on the troublemakers within his party as hard as he could have done; but then the main culprits were senior players who should have known better. The inexperienced tourists merely followed the example of their elders and supposedly betters and the visitors degenerated into a bunch of sour-faced, aggressive tourists, not New Zealand's usual Rugby ambassadors.

Kirkpatrick's behaviour throughout was

Ian Kirkpatrick, shadowed by fly-half Bob Burgess, is New Zealand's leading try-scorer of all time, with sixteen in thirty-nine Tests.

Ian Kirkpatrick, Rugby's leading international try-scoring forward, about to add another in the 1971 game between England and the President's XV, as part of the RFU's centenary celebrations.

impeccable, and he hoped that his charges would follow his example; but they did not, the tour aged him and his form suffered. All tours of that length require senior, responsible players in authority, which is why Colin Meads would have been an invaluable member of the seventh All Blacks. That Ian Kirkpatrick maintained his high standards throughout showed his sincere and thought-ful temperament; he had a right to have expected more of his colleagues.

He captained the All Blacks in their home defeat by England in 1973, and there were questions about his leadership when the party to tour Australia was being selected. But lack of other candidates for the captaincy seemed like being 'Kirkie's' saviour, yet Andy Leslie was named skipper of the touring party, with the selectors pointing out that he had been chosen as a player first, then picked to lead. Ian Kirkpatrick took his demise with his usual dignity and proceeded to give his all for the new All Black captain. And with the pressure off, the flanker was back to his best form with some exceptional displays on the New Zealand tour to Ireland, England and Wales in 1974.

New Zealand's only game in 1975 was the 'water polo' Test against Scotland and the succeeding years saw Kirkpatrick play a full part in the series against South Africa and the British Lions. His run of thirty-eight consecutive internationals was broken when he was not selected to tour France at the end of 1977. It was the finish of his international career – coach Jack Gleeson was intent on blooding youngsters on the tour and felt that Ian Kirkpatrick's playing contribution to international Rugby was over, although neither Gleeson or anyone else in Rugby doubted the immense contribution of this world-class flanker. It is for that contribution as a player, rather than as a captain, that Ian Kirkpatrick will be remembered.

Jackie Kyle

The Irishman John Kyle, known as Jackie, was the first in a long and exceptional line of talented British fly-halves. An instant success when he first appeared on the international scene in 1947, Kyle set a standard for all to follow. He was very much a canny player who would wait for the opposing defence to relax and think that he was having an off day; if necessary, he would wait for seventy-nine minutes and then, with the defence congratulating itself that its task had been accomplished successfully that day, Kyle would seize his chance and the game for his side.

His international career spanned eleven seasons, but that element of surprise and the unexpected remained throughout. His mastery of the fly-half arts was complete; he attacked with the ball in his hands and through his tactical kicking – his intuitive assessment of the situation was immaculate. And unlike many running fly-halves, Kyle was happy and effective in the rough and tumble of defence, whether tackling or positioning himself perfectly to collect a supposedly probing kick ahead. A slightly-built man, he proved, nevertheless, Ireland's most potent attacking force for over a decade and such was his dual style of attacking play that he was known as 'The Ghost' in France and, after the 1950 Lions' visit, 'The Twins' in New Zealand. In his lengthy career with Ireland, he had the distinction of playing with eight different scrum-halves, beginning with Ray Carroll in 1947 and finishing with Andy Mulligan in the 1958 season. By the time Jackie Kyle had retired from international football, his forty-six caps were a world record (since passed).

It was John (not Jackie) Wilson Kyle that the future Irish fly-half was christened in 1926; and he was born into a typically sporting Irish family. Kyle's other main sports, first at Belfast Royal Academy, then at Queen's University, were cricket and boxing. His early Rugby was played at centre and full-back, but he moved to fly-half one day at Queen's when the first choice was unavailable. He had gone to Queen's in 1943 to study as a medical student and the move brought him in contact with Ernie Strathdee: the pair were later to play together at half-back for Ireland. Although Kyle won forty-six caps, he turned out for Ireland fifty-one times, playing in five unofficial games against the British Army and the other countries in the international championship just after the war. He made his first official appearance in the match versus France in 1947 and, apart from injury, was in the Ireland team for the next eleven years. His happiest memory of his first full international season was the 22-0 drubbing of England at Dublin.

That triumph was to herald a golden era of Irish Rugby; in fact, their finest yet. Three of the next four championships were theirs – 1948, 1949 and 1951; those first two years were also Triple Crown years and 1948 also signalled Ireland's one and only Grand

Jackie Kyle clears upfield for Ireland in their game against England at Lansdowne Road in 1957.

Slam. (Their next championship title was under the leadership of Willie John McBride in 1974.) One of Kyle's most notable games in this period was the battle against Wales at Swansea in 1949, the last time these two countries played there. Ireland won 5-0 and their only try took place when Kyle sneaked round the blind-side and chipped over the defence for McCarthy to steal the winning score under the noses of the Welsh defence. Accusations of 'robbery' were often laid at the door of Kyle's genius.

In between Ireland's hat-tricks of triumphs, Kyle travelled to New Zealand with the 1950 British Lions. His all-round performances brought him rave notices wherever he played and his form in the Test series was outstanding. In the opening Test, he scored a brilliant individual try and then made another one for Wales's wing Ken Jones in the nine-all draw. Although the All Blacks won the remaining three Tests, Kyle's place among the great British backs that the New Zealand crowds love and revere was assured. His jinky running was all the more admirable in the days when backs were not allowed the freedom they have today. The All Blacks were quick to acknowledge the presence of one of the most complete footballers to have visited their islands and he was the star among a talented

Jackie Kyle, the first in a long line of brilliant post-war fly-halves who have represented the British Lions with distinction.

bunch of British backs. Like Gibson after him, Jackie Kyle was held up as the perfect example for aspiring New Zealand backs to follow.

Although Kyle returned to help his country to one more championship, the golden days for Irish Rugby were over and neither Kyle nor Ireland were to enjoy again the success of those early years. But he was still more than capable of dominating and winning internationals. When Kyle lined up against Wales in Dublin in 1956, the men in green had not beaten the Principality since that historic day at Swansea in 1949. A record crowd crammed into Lansdowne Road to see its favourite fly-half inspire Ireland to an 11-6 victory. And it was a memorable day for another reason – included in those eleven points was a dropped goal by JW Kyle, his first and last for Ireland in forty-six internationals. He

bowed out of top-class Rugby after the 1958 game with Scotland, which fittingly Ireland won 12-6; it was the only proper way in which this talented player could depart the scene he had graced so expertly all those years.

At the age of thirty-two, Jackie Kyle was the most-capped Rugby player in the history of the game. In addition to his forty-six Irish caps, he had also played in six Tests for the British Lions and his influence had a profound effect on fly-halves. Even the intuitive Cliff Morgan owed much of his game, especially with regard to cover defence, to this talented Irishman, who had dominated Rugby for more than a decade.

Chris Laidlaw

The finest footballing scrum-half produced by New Zealand since the war, Chris Laidlaw's skills and Rugby brain usually won him selection over the more individual and dogged Sid Going when the pair were in contention for the All Blacks' jersey.

Laidlaw made his first major New Zealand tour when he was only nineteen, evidence of his considerable promise and the high hopes the selectors had of him. There was no doubting his prodigious talents and, as well as being a top-class performer in his own right, Laidlaw was a player who brought out the best in his fly-half and three-quarters. This blond scrum-half, who stood five foot nine and weighed just under thirteen stone, was able to adapt his game to the opposition's strengths and weaknesses. The facet of his game which will always be remembered by Rugby fans all over the world was his long, spiralling spin pass, which was so effective in either direction; it set the trend for scrum-halves everywhere including the likes of Wales' Gareth Edwards and Scotland's Alan Lawson.

Laidlaw was a serious-minded person,

Chris Laidlaw, who was outstanding on Lochore's 1967 All Blacks' tour, kicks ahead in the international against England.

who followed a scholastic career during his reign as All Blacks' scrum-half; he came out strongly against the apartheid system when he toured South Africa with New Zealand in 1970, although Colin Meads felt that Laidlaw had visited there quite deliberately to look for the bad. That tour saw his final appearance as an All Black; although only twenty-seven, it had always been obvious that here was an All Black for whom Rugby was not life and death. Laidlaw had played twenty times for New Zealand in internationals and is the most-capped All Black scrum-half behind Going.

Born in 1943, Chris Robert Laidlaw was educated at the King's High School, Dunedin and, while he was studying at Otago University, went straight into the Otago provincial side from school. He was one of the newcomers in Wilson Whineray's 1963–64 party that toured Britain and France, and was competing for the scrum-half Test spot with the experienced Briscoe. The youngster started well, gaining the edge, but

Chris Laidlaw, shown playing for Oxford University, spent two years there and captained them to victory over the 1969-70 Springboks.

a poor performance against Cardiff, perhaps unfairly, put him out of the running for the international against Ireland. This affected his confidence badly, becoming upset by the apparent sink-or-swim attitude of skipper Whineray. With Briscoe playing well, Laidlaw's displays became erratic and by the middle of the visit seemed headed for oblivion. Eventually, he clawed his way back and, with Briscoe showing poor form

against Scotland, the scrum-half place was up for grabs again. Laidlaw needed no second asking; his confidence soared as the magic touch returned. In three successive games at the end of the tour – against France B, France and the Barbarians – his long passing and poised running suddenly had critics hailing him as one of the stars on the visit. In his first international – against France – the new scrum-half dropped a goal to ensure the All Blacks' 12-3 victory.

Laidlaw had arrived as a world-class player and, later that year, led the New Zealand Colts to Japan before becoming a regular member of the full All Black team. He was now playing behind an All Black pack which was reaching its peak; indeed, in the series against the 1965 Springboks and the 1966 British Lions, there were claims that the scrum-half could have sat in an arm-chair, so perfect was the protection and quality of ball provided by those eight New Zealand forwards. After those successful internationals, Laidlaw was now facing his first challenge from Sid Going and the pair toured Britain and France under Brian Lochore in 1967; rarely can a touring party have had such a wealth of talent at scrum-half. Laidlaw did not always show his best form during the tour, but remained number one throughout, although Going was brought into the French game as a 'one-off' to disrupt the opposition. Going complained that no matter how well he played – and he made the same complaints in South Africa in 1970 – he was not going to get into the Test side above Laidlaw. That is probably true; Freddie Allen's expansive style of running Rugby needed a link man of the quality of Chris Laidlaw, not the brilliant individualistic talent of Sid Going.

The following year in 1968, Laidlaw cap-tained the All Blacks in a game against the Wallabies when Lochore was injured, but later in 1968 a broken thumb kept the scrum-half out of the third Test against France and Going came in to score two tries. Laidlaw was also missing from the two games against Wales in 1969.

He was away at the time, having travelled on a Rhodes Scholarship to Oxford Univer-sity where his influence and captaincy helped the 'Dark Blues' to a memorable 6–3 victory over Dawie de Villiers' Springboks at Twickenham in late 1969; a few weeks later they also won the 'Varsity match.

He came back to New Zealand in 1970 to claim his place in the trials and, again, it was Laidlaw and Going who travelled with the All Blacks to South Africa. Laidlaw was replaced by Going during the first Test when the former was concussed, but re-turned for the next two internationals, and scored his third and final All Black try in the second Test. A burst appendix left the way open for Going in the final game and Chris Laidlaw's international career was over. Laidlaw's fly-half in that third game was his Otago University team-mate Earle Kirton and the pair played together nine times for New Zealand.

Chris Laidlaw's illustrious career had ended prematurely, as many thought it might; Rugby, not even All Black Rugby, was not going to dominate his life as it had done others. He wrote a controversial best-seller, *Mud in Your Eye* – the title sums up the book's attitude perfectly – which was an analysis of the game based on his All Black experience and his Rugby travels, including his days at Oxford and later playing Rugby in France. It did not win him many friends among New Zealand Rugby administrators, and he never thought that it might.

Arguments will continue forever about the respective merits of Laidlaw and Going. Both were exceptionally fine players, but it is worth noting that when Freddie Allen wanted a scrum-half to make the best use of the ball won by that frightening All Black eight, he chose Chris Laidlaw as the man they should give it to, knowing that he would make maximum use of it.

Willie John McBride

Seldom has a Rugby career been split into two such differing halves, with success following on from disappointment, as that of Willie John McBride. When Willie John left Ellis Park, South Africa, in 1968 after the fourth Test between the Springboks and the British Lions, he could easily be forgiven for thinking of calling it a day. It was his third Lions' tour and his ninth Test appear-ance . . . and he was still waiting for his first win! His career with Ireland, with whom he had been a regular since 1962, had not provided him with too many successes either.

Not that these defeats were without their beneficial effects. Scores had to be settled and, some way or another, the southern hemisphere Rugby giants were going to suffer. For too long they had looked upon British forwards with contempt, regarding their lack of competitiveness and physical aggression as a weakness. McBride did, too, and by 1968 he had had enough of being pushed around by successive Springbok and All Blacks' packs. It was time to get out or do something about it.

So when as pack leader he led the forwards to victory in the 1971 series against New Zealand and then, as captain, he drove the Lions to complete the most devastating humiliation of a home side in an international series, in South Africa in 1974, he attained a sense of joy and fulfilment granted to few men in Rugby or any walk of life.

To understand the satisfaction felt by this Ballymena man, it is necessary to recall those early setbacks and consider their effect on a very intelligent player, whose love of Rugby sprang from the physical nature of the game and the comradeship that was created from devotion to a single cause. Brought up on a farm, his father had died when he was four. His mother had to bring up four boys and a girl and the single-mindedness with which she set about this task had a profound effect on Willie John. Sacrifices had to be made, and all through his career he expected sacrifices to be made in attempting any goal.

Willie John McBride on the attack in a match against France.

Perhaps because he was usually needed at home or because he preferred athletics, he was a late starter as far as Rugby was concerned; not, in fact, until his second last year at Ballymena Academy. Within three weeks of playing a house match just before Christmas 1957, he was in the school first fifteen. After the New Year, he appeared for Ulster Schools against Munster and a report at the time commented: 'McBride was the

But McBride had caught the bug and he joined Ballymena when he left school. That move brought him into contact with a player who was to influence McBride greatly. They were later to share many triumphs together, as Ballymena did under their guidance. The other half to the partnership was Ireland's international prop Syd Millar.

The raw newcomer quickly made the first fifteen and in 1960 had his first taste of the big time when he was selected for Ulster against Avril Malan's Springbok side. It was a testing baptism for the young McBride as he was matched against Johann Claassen, one of the finest locks in the world at that time. McBride remembers his introduction to the big time: 'He was tough, strong and much too experienced for me. Yet I never saw him do anything dirty – he was too good a player and only interested in the ball. He was outstanding against me in the rucks, mauls and line-outs.'

But McBride was making his mark and he was one of nine new caps picked for the 1962 game against England at Twickenham. Unfortunately, Richard Sharp was at his very best that day and McBride's debut was marked by a 16-0 defeat. The raw youngster kept his place for the rest of the season and even a broken leg in the final game against France did not spoil his chances of selection for the Lions' tour to South Africa that summer. He had broken his left fibia, but returned after ten minutes to complete the game with his leg strapped up.

The injury meant that he did not appear on the Lions' tour until the sixth match, but improved enough in form to displace Keith Rowlands for the third and fourth Tests. McBride's partner in the second row was Bill 'Wigs' Mulcahy, who had kept an eye on the young Ulsterman since they had

biggest boy on the field, but certainly not the best.' Well, even in those days it was difficult for a lock forward to outshine the likes of David Hewitt and Tom Kiernan who were also playing in the match.

played together for Ireland. The South Africans had clinched that series in the dying minutes of the third game.

McBride was again to be on the losing side four years later with Mike Campbell-Lamerton's Lions in New Zealand. McBride had proved himself a tough, competitive force on these tours, but he felt humiliated by the whitewash of 1966. He sensed that many of his colleagues were demoralised and beaten even before they took the field. The New Zealanders impressed McBride and such was the force of their Rugby that he would have dearly loved to have played just one game for the All Blacks. He recalls: 'The way I looked at it was that if New Zealand had something to teach – which they had – then I was willing to learn. When I first played in New Zealand I couldn't believe it. I had played in South Africa, of course, but here was something different. It was a real man's game. There was no quarter asked or given and that was the way every game was played, wherever we went. The emphasis was in the right place – on the character of the men who played the game.' Unfortunately, there were not enough of McBride's team-mates who felt the same way.

That 1966 tour brought McBride into contact for the second time with a man identified as much with All Black Rugby as McBride is with Irish and British Rugby. That man was Colin Meads and his many battles with McBride had begun at Lansdowne Road during Whineray's 1963-64 tour, and ended eight years later, the day British Rugby, and McBride, at last won something.

In that first contest, which Ireland were unlucky to lose 5-6, they tested out each other's physical commitment to the game. Once that was established, they competed with each other on equal terms for nearly the next decade, an equality born out of tremendous respect for each other's character and Rugby; to McBride, Meads was the complete forward.

McBride gave of his best again in 1968, when the Lions were touring South Africa. But, although there were signs of a change in administration for the better, three Tests were lost with the other drawn. Yet the veteran of over 30 caps felt that a breakthrough had been made, and this gave him the strength to keep going.

Up to that tour, McBride had only missed one game for his country since his debut, when the selectors made the choice, which now seems sacrilegious, of naming Mick Leahy in his place at second row for the game against Wales in 1964. That error was soon realised and from that day until his retirement from the international scene in 1975, there was always a place for WJ McBride in the second row for Ireland.

And playing for his country gave him his first chance of walking off the field in an overseas international a winner. The year was 1967 and the place Australia. It was his first tour abroad with Ireland and they celebrated in fine style, winning the international 11-5 in teriffic heat at Sydney. It was also the first time any of the four home countries had recorded a Test win in the southern hemisphere.

Although he had earlier wondered at the wisdom of returning to New Zealand in 1971, where he had been so humiliated five years earlier, the attitude and determination of the management convinced him this was no bunch of losers. McBride was only going back to New Zealand to win. The combination of Doug Smith, Carwyn James and John Dawes, plus the influence of Irish prop Ray McLoughlin, vanquished any fears that McBride might have had about this being another British side going to the slaughter.

There was already talk of the veteran lock being over the hill, but these accusations came from the uninitiated, who did not understand the vital role McBride was to fulfil. And, after the battle at Canterbury, a week before the opening Test, he found his responsibilities had increased. Both the first-choice props, Sandy Carmichael and

Willie John McBride being chaired by Lions colleagues after clinching the series against South Africa in 1974.

pack leader Ray McLoughlin, were injured and had to be sent home. So, with only a few days to the most important game of the tour, Willie John was given the job of uniting the forwards including the two new props, Ian McLauchlan and Sean Lynch. If that game was lost, then all that McBride had worked for would be gone for ever; there were going to be no second chances this time. He had to instil this into the players, making sure they were mentally, as well as physically, prepared for the contest.

It is just as well they were, because the New Zealand forwards were in top gear that afternoon. But the British defence held out as wave upon wave of black shirts bore down on them. The Lions led 9-3 through an Ian McLauchlan try and Barry John's goal-kicking, and with Barry John tantalising New Zealand full-back Fergie McCormick with his inch-perfect tactical kicking the day belonged to the Lions, and to Willie John in particular. It was a moment he will always cherish: 'I shall never forget how I felt after that match. I had endured the humiliations of 1966, so to win a Test in

New Zealand gave me indescribable pleasure. Now we knew Carwyn was right, we really could take this series, but it would be a long, hard road.'

And what a moment for McBride when Colin Meads walked into the Lions' dressing room after the game and offered his jersey to the Lion. But this Ulsterman knew the series was a long way from being over. The next night when the team settled down to watch a recording of that first Test, McBride slowly got up, said: 'That's all history now, lads' and walked out of the room to take his pleasures elsewhere. It had taken him too long and there had been too much heartache on the way for him to be carried away on the wave of this one success.

His influence on the other members of the touring party was very important. His appeal was simple and straightforward—he led by example with total commitment and he expected the same from those around him. Off the field, his commitment was the same—a hundred per cent. A fine singer of ballads, a tremendous entertainer and a mature, intelligent and sensible outlook on Rugby and life.

The British Lions lost that second Test—their only defeat in New Zealand on that tour—so victory in the third game was vital. The Lions, with the all-Welsh back-row of Derek Quinnell, Mervyn Davies and John Taylor snuffing out the threat of Sid Going, responded magnificently. And McBride reckons that the first twenty-five minutes of that Test contained the finest Rugby in which he had ever played. Those opening minutes gave the visitors a 13-0 lead and the All Blacks never recovered.

Now the Lions could not lose the series and they eventually fulfilled the prophesy of manager Doug Smith by winning two, losing one and drawing the other. For Willie John McBride, it was a dream come true: 'I will never forget the final whistle in Auckland. At last the Lions had won something and reliving it all was tremendous—the battle of Canterbury, where we lost

virtually an entire front-row; the determination of Lynch and Ian McLauchlan as they stood up to the might of a New Zealand pack in the first Test; the dedication of men at last inspired to giving their last ounce in scrums, line-out, maul and ruck, never mind the tackling in defence; the cheek and confidence of Barry John and Mike Gibson—and of course the coolness and control of John Dawes and JPR Williams at full-back.'

Having returned from New Zealand a winner, was this the time for McBride to retire? He had won something at last. But in many ways, he was only just beginning to reap the rewards for all those defeats in the sixties. He played for Ireland in their 10-10 draw with Ian Kirkpatrick's All Blacks and midway through the 1973 International Championship, he took over the captaincy of his country when Tom Kiernan finally departed. That was the year all the countries tied with two wins and two defeats each. The captaincy brought him into partnership with Syd Millar again, who was the national coach, and it was to prove a profitable relationship for the pair. Not only did they bring Ireland the International Championship in 1974—their first for 23 years—later that year they combined as captain and coach of the 1974 Lions' tour to South Africa.

At thirty-three years of age, McBride had his critics about whether he was the right choice to lead the Lions against the Springboks. No-one was doubting his credentials—only his stamina to fulfil the exacting duties of leading twenty-nine other players. On the plus side, with Syd Millar as coach, it was merely an extension of the combination that had led Ireland to success. And this harmony between captain and coach had been a crucial factor in the success in New Zealand in 1971.

McBride believed that it was the coach's job to take charge of training, tactics and preparing players for matches. He saw his own task in terms of motivating his side on the day of the game. He dedicated himself to success in the matches. He made sacrifices and he expected his players to do the same, because there was no other way to win. McBride had always been a player's man and his players in 1974 responded by being prepared to 'die' for their captain. They would do anything not to let him down; they respected him and they wanted his respect, and they would only earn that the hard way, by showing complete dedication to the cause. Bill McBride never had any time for 'small' men. He commanded total loyalty.

But even he could not have foreseen the way the Lions steamrollered through South African Rugby. It was the perfect culmination to a career that had seen British Rugby grow up, and McBride had played a larger part than most in the maturing process. That Lions' pack of 1974 must lay claims to being one of the finest groups of forwards of all time, both individually and collectively. Their control was complete and such was their domination that the side ran in ten tries in the Test series.

South African Rugby has never been on the receiving end of such a battering. And, after all the work that had gone into the success, McBride was not going to allow the Springboks to intimidate their way back into the series. This led to the renowned '99' call sign, which meant one in, all in, if there was any trouble. McBride had all too often found himself isolated from support and help on previous Lions' tours; he realised the paramount need for unity at these times. July 13, at Port Elizabeth, was probably McBride's greatest day. His side, for the third time, had seen off the Springbok challenge and the series was theirs, and his. McBride had seen his career come full circle. He had earned his rewards the hard way. He had given himself totally to the tour, and his players had given themselves totally to him. The veteran had paced himself, sleeping in the afternoons to conserve his energy; he played some of the finest Rugby of his long career. His presence had been enough to motivate players like Gareth Edwards, Fergus Slattery and Gordon Brown to new heights. Although the final game was drawn, the Lions' record of twenty-one wins in twenty-two games is unparalleled in modern times; all the more impressive because it was a definite case of men against boys. A phrase McBride may have recalled from earlier in his career, though not referring to the same sides.

He returned to play one more season for Ireland, setting a world-record of sixty-three appearances when he retired, plus another seventeen Test appearances for the Lions. Unfortunately, in his last game, his side met a top-form Welsh fifteen at Cardiff Arms Park and they trounced the Irish 32-4. McBride knew that the time had come to retire.

But in that last season he collected a first for his country and, fittingly, it was in his last international appearance at Lansdowne Road. Towards the end of that game against France, Willie John was making one of his customary charges. This time it took him over the French line for his first-ever try for Ireland. Lansdowne Road went mad. They, too, knew what a hell of a man Willie John was. They, like us, responded to his dedication, his skill and his undying love of Rugby.

Ian McLauchlan

A pocket-battleship prop, Ian McLauchlan had the ability to combat the Rugby giants of New Zealand and South Africa in the seventies and crush them unmercifully. A product of the McBride school of thought that nothing is gained without sacrifice and dedication, his position as one of the great Scottish and Lions' props and characters is assured. McLauchlan was a founder-member of the new-breed British forwards, who would not allow himself to be intimidated by the bully boys of the southern hemisphere and for whom the physical con-

Ian McLauchlan bears down on the East Midlands'
fly-half while playing for the Barbarians. Behind
him is Alastair McHarg, a fellow member of
Scotland's pack on many occasions.

frontation is a necessary and important part
of the game. A hundredpercenter who
answered the call of his country when it was
in trouble in 1971 he stayed around for the
rest of the decade.

It took him six years from his first trial
until he took the field in a Scottish jersey . . .
it was a long and unfair wait, with Rugby
nearly losing him to ski-ing, but, once in, he
dedicated himself to the cause of Scottish
Rugby, and became the figurehead for
Scotland's Rugby hopes in the seventies.
Twice, he was heartbroken to see his
country's Triple Crown hopes trampled by
the English into the mud of Twickenham.

As captain, his enthusiasm carried Scotland through what may otherwise have been a sticky patch; once his leadership had gone, the Scottish team lost their way again. He has a fairly ruthless approach to Rugby, and life in general, but all that was channelled into a single cause when he was leading his country. Because of this, he was able to unite the normal wayward and individual Scottish temperament as few have done before.

In 1977, McLauchlan was discarded by the Scots and the British Lions. The Scots were able to redeem themselves and offer him his old place back, but his vast experience was sadly missed on the Lions' tour of New Zealand. Instead, he spent the latter part of the summer touring Japan with the Scottish squad. It was Nairn MacEwan's first assignment as coach and a young and inexperienced party was taken to the Far East. The 'old man's' attitude in helping younger players was exemplary and he found a great deal of pleasure in passing on his wealth of experience to those at the start of their international careers; he filled the role of elder statesman on that tour with distinction. Not that he was ready to bow out just yet—the young pretenders found he was not going to abdicate without a fight.

And John 'Ian' McLauchlan had been a fighter all his days. His school days were spent at Ayr Academy, where he played in the first fifteen for four seasons on the flank, as well as representing Glasgow Schools. When he left, he went to study at Jordanhill College and came under the influence of Bill Dickenson, the man who was to become his mentor in many ways. Not that Dickenson's words were that encouraging to the new arrival. He told him that he was not fast enough or strong enough to play flanker in senior Rugby. He advised him to take up weight-training, which McLauchlan did with his usual singlemindedness; he progressed from eleven stone four to thirteen stone ten in three months. Then Ian McLauchlan took his first steps to becoming a world-class prop and was soon appearing in Jordanhill's first fifteen at loose-head; there quickly followed calls to play for the Glasgow District side.

But at five foot nine, he was already being ridiculed as being too small to compete at the top level as a prop. It was probably a factor in his long wait for a cap. When first called up for a trial in 1963, he caused the then skipper Michael Campbell-Lamerton much consternation as he tried to work out the newcomer's position—prop being the last of the skipper's suggestions. Although he showed promise, the selectors were sceptical about his ability of being able to overcome his lack of inches; it took six years for the doubts to fade and for McLauchlan to gain a very hard-earned cap.

The player himself was determined to show them that he had been kept on the sidelines too long and, apart from being dropped in 1970 after a defeat by Wales at Cardiff, he became a fixture in the Scottish side. He toured the Argentine with Scotland in 1970, partnering Sandy Carmichael in a prop pairing that was to rival Hughie McLeod and David Rollo in Scotland legend. Both were selected for the 1971 Lions' tour, Carmichael being the number one tight-head, and McLauchlan the number two loose-head to Ray McLoughlin, the Irishman who was to play a large part in that team's success. McLauchlan was horrified at the battering Carmichael took in the Canterbury game a week before the opening Test. Also injured in that game was Ray McLoughlin and both front-line props had to leave the tour, although McLoughlin's influence was to last throughout. It left Ian McLauchlan and Sean Lynch to take on the might of the All Blacks the following Saturday.

New Zealand critics had rated the pair as too small for international Rugby and when the Lions came up with the nickname of 'Mighty Mouse' for the Scot, 'Mickey Mouse' was the Kiwi response. But, as he burrowed under giant tight-head after tight-head, the lack of inches which had been ridiculed suddenly became his strength; and such was his propping ability, he was able, as he himself describes, to pop them like corks from a bottle. The 'Mickey Mouse' cracks became fewer and fewer as the country which prides itself on its forward power came to appreciate this 'giant's' ability and technique. McLauchlan and Sean Lynch proved themselves to the world—they already knew themselves how good they were—in the four Tests, helping the Lions to victory in the series. McLauchlan gained great pleasure from scoring the only try in the opening Test, although he had never been adverse to doing this in the past—another attribute of the new-style prop.

For the international prop, strength was no longer enough; you had to be skilled in the techniques of propping and there were few men to rival Ian McLauchlan. He obviously benefited greatly on this tour from the influence of Ray McLoughlin. The Scot had been worried that he would spend the whole tour as reserve to the Irishman, for whom he had tremendous respect—'to beat him, you'd have to kill him' McLauchlan admitted. But McLoughlin's role was played mainly off the field and it was McLauchlan who gained the glory and satisfaction of knowing he was now amongst the best.

In 1973, he took over the captaincy of Scotland, whom he led for nineteen matches. It was an eventful first season for the prop. In his opening game in charge, the Welsh were defeated at Murrayfield; the Scots forwards' tactics of marching the scrum sideways disturbed the Welsh, who once again failed to beat the Murrayfield bogey.

In the following game, against Ireland at Murrayfield, the new captain broke his right tibia and was carried off just before half-time, but the Scots won and travelled to Twickenham to attempt to win their first Triple Crown since 1938. The 'Mouse's'

powers of recovery are quicker than most, but perhaps it would have been better if he had missed this one. Yet, his presence was so important to his team that he took a calculated risk. It was a gamble that didn't come off; the Scots played well below par and yet another Scottish Triple Crown attempt was buried in the mud of Headquarters. But with McLauchlan at the helm and Dickenson as coach, the Scottish pack were becoming the best bunch of forwards in the Championship.

However, only two other members of that pack were selected to go with McLauchlan and the Lions to South Africa in 1974—Carmichael and lock Gordon Brown, both of whom had been with him in New Zealand three years earlier. But McLauchlan was never to play in a Test with his great partner Sandy Carmichael; his front-row companions on this tour being Welshman hooker Bobby 'Duke' Windsor and Englishman Fran Cotton.

McLauchlan had always found that opposing British tight-heads gave him far more trouble than those from the southern hemisphere. He felt that the Springboks used the scrum just to restart the game and were far too upright in their stance. McLaughlan regards the scrum as a vital part of the game, as do most players in this country. He had noted a tremendous decline in their forward play, since he won his second cap against the Springboks at Murrayfield in 1969, when he found them a big and good scrummaging side. But he thought that in 1974 they were terrible, or appeared so, as the British scrummaging had improved by leaps and bounds.

This front-row, unbalanced in height only, became one of the popular features of the tour and a great favourite with the crowds. They provided a basis for an unbeaten tour. McLauchlan had now visited the two former strongholds of forward power and had proved himself their master. He enjoyed the second Lions' tour more because he was a senior member, given more

Scotland's captain Ian McLauchlan at the front of a line-out in the 1975 game against the Wallabies at Murrayfield.

responsibility and a larger part in the coaching.

The following year brought about another bid on the Triple Crown. And again he ran onto the turf of Twickenham with two-thirds of the Crown achieved. But the

Scots, who had been playing well, again fell victim to the Twickenham hoodoo and another chance went a-begging. He toured New Zealand that summer of '75, but any hopes of victory were drowned in the only 'water polo' Test. He returned for his final international season as captain, although he did not know it at the time. Scotland beat Australia, England and Ireland, but lost to Wales and France. With ten wins in nineteen matches, he has been one of Scotland's most successful captains, and certainly one of the most popular. Their record at Murrayfield was almost invincible, with nine wins out of eleven – and their record away from Scotland has always been lamentable.

The Scottish selectors then decided that McLauchlan was 'over the hill' and he was dropped from the captaincy and the side for the 1977 game against England at Twickenham; it was a grave error of judgement. It was cruel of the selectors to deny the prop the chance of revenge over the 'auld enemy'. With no adequate replacement forthcoming, the Scots were hammered and the selectors back to square one. By the end of the season, McLauchlan was back in the side, though not as captain. Still, he helped Scotland to their best performance of the season against Wales. It was probably a performance which should have earned him a Lions' tour to New Zealand, but it did not.

Yet, as the seventies neared their close, there was no real sign of a successor and he was still occupying his place in the national side. His influence, whatever position in the side he had, was considerable and he commanded a rare loyalty from his players when leading the side. He returned as captain for the 1979 game against New Zealand. That he proved everyone wrong who had joked about his size is undeniable and he emerged as one of the strongest personalities in world Rugby in the seventies.

Ray McLoughlin sets up quality ball for his scrum-half, John Moloney, in Ireland's game against the 1973 Argentinians.

Ray McLoughlin

One of the greatest thinking forwards of his or any era, Ray McLoughlin's career was split into two halves as he waited for his philosophies to be accepted. They say that a prophet is never accepted in his own land and there is some truth in this in McLoughlin's case. As a radical captain, he reorganised Irish thinking in 1965, but despite almost leading his team to the Triple

Crown, his methods were soon rejected and with them, his chance of leading the 1966 Lions to New Zealand.

After eighteen caps for Ireland, McLoughlin was away from the international scene for five years before returning in 1971 to find that his teachings were finding some favour and he was able to make an important contribution to the success of the 1971 British Lions. It was not a question of this loose-head prop returning to the fold, rather that the thinking of players and administrators was now along the same lines as McLoughlin's; it had taken them a long time to come round.

Born in 1939, Raymond John McLoughlin spent some of his early Rugby days at full-back, centre and fly-half while playing for Garbally College, Ballinasloe, but he was at prop when studying at University College, Dublin. It was McBride's first cap the day that McLoughlin also made his debut, against England at Twickenham in 1962. The pair suffered defeat, which was something not uncommon to those wearing the green jersey at that time. Three years later in 1965, while playing for Gosforth, the prop was asked to lead his country; it was nothing unusual for McLoughlin that season as he also led Gosforth, Northumberland, Connacht and the British Universities. His captaincy saw the end of Ireland's rather carefree attitude to international Rugby. McLoughlin knew that there was a need for a change in the approach and thinking of the Irish national team; his approach was based on thoroughness, total commitment and a much greater application than had previously been shown. Training sessions became much harder and time was spent analysing the strengths and weaknesses of the opposition.

In March of his first season in charge, he took Ireland to the Arms Park as both countries strove for the Triple Crown. It was the first time in fifty-four years that there had been a real Triple Crown 'decider' – but the day belonged to Wales and for the tenth time in their history, they denied Ireland the Triple Crown at the final hurdle.

McLoughlin's critics were only looking for defeat as an excuse to attack his meticulous methods. Two losses and a draw in 1966 gave them the ammunition they needed and the captaincy passed to Tom Kiernan. Many felt that McLoughlin's rule was too inflexible and his system could not work considering the players he had at his disposal. Perhaps he merely tried too much too soon.

105

The prop had looked a strong challenger for the Lions' captaincy, but had to be content with a place in Mike Campbell-Lamerton's party as their first-choice loose-head prop. It was an 'up-and-down' tour for him; after showing top form in Australia where he played in the two successful internationals against the Wallabies, he had to withdraw for the opening two Tests against the All Blacks because of hamstring trouble. But there was a place in the front-row for him in the magnificent fourth Test victory; in fact, he had played in the three winning internationals on that tour.

There followed five years in the wilderness as cartilage and other injuries and his studies took him around Britain, keeping him out of the limelight. Clubs he played for during this period included London Irish, Athlone, Gosforth and Blackrock College. He may be forgiven for thinking that his tally of eighteen caps would not be improved on. Returning to Dublin and work at the Irish Industrial Development Authority, McLoughlin found his roots again and returned to the national fifteen in 1971. His performances proved that he had lost none of his strength, technique and skill, so at the age of thirty-one, he set off on his second Lions' tour, again to New Zealand.

Along with coach Carwyn James,

Ray McLoughlin, who toured New Zealand twice with the Lions, bursts through against France in 1972 during his second 'spell' in the Ireland national side.

McLoughlin worked out the forward strategy for the series against the All Blacks. The prop wanted to know when Barry John was going to kick into the 'box' or spin the ball, so that his pack could give them maximum support. The scene was set for a thrilling contest, but McLoughlin's battle came a week too soon when he broke a thumb retaliating in the Canterbury game. It was also the match in which Sandy Carmichael suffered a multiple fracture of his cheekbone and so both first-choice test props had to return home. The decision to send McLoughlin back was looked upon by many as rather hasty. But his presence remained throughout the tour, if only in spirit, and the two replacement props, Ian McLauchlan and Sean Lynch, became heroes of the historic victory.

Back for Ireland in 1972, Ray McLoughlin scored one of his rare tries, but one of the most memorable for Ireland, charging over with several French defenders hanging on to him. It helped give the Irish their first win in Paris for twenty years. It had looked a likely Grand Slam for Ireland that year, with two away wins, but the political trouble there meant that the home fixtures with Scotland and Wales were not played.

Still, two years later, Ray McLoughlin was one of the veterans of the Irish side – 'Dad's Army' someone nicknamed the side containing Willie John McBride, Ken Kennedy, Mike Gibson, Sean Lynch – who won their first championship for twenty-three years. The day the title was theirs, Ireland were not playing and watched with joy as, against the odds, England and Scotland beat Wales and France. This win gave several players the impetus to carry on, but after their drubbing by Wales, 32-4, at the end of the 1975 season, McLoughlin and McBride had had enough. The lock retired with a then world-record of sixty-three caps

and McLoughlin at prop had played forty times for Ireland, a record in his position for Ireland. Both had served their country and the Lions well. Ray McLoughlin was rated one of the most knowledgeable and strongest props ever seen, but this deep thinker on the game of Rugby will also always be remembered for his immense contribution to Irish and British Rugby off the field of play.

Jo Maso

Talented French midfield player Jo Maso found more favour with supporters everywhere than with his own selectors, who

The talented French centre, Jo Maso, whose skills found much more favour with the general Rugby supporter than his own national selectors.

showed a distinct lack of appreciation of his many abilities. He was in and out of the national side all through his seven-year international career and was finally discarded in 1973, long before his considerable powers were on the wane. Maso was a centre in the fine French tradition with a liking for the unorthodox, rare footballing skills and exceptional vision; his style and build were often compared to André Boniface and many saw Maso as his natural successor in the national side.

Jo Maso may have been neglected by the French selectors on some occasions, but English crowds saw him in fine form when playing for the World XV during England's centenary celebrations in 1971.

Some of Maso's international days were spent at fly-half, where he also showed great promise, and there was much controversy about where he was better suited and more useful to the side, that is if he found favour with the French selectors. While a fine performer at fly-half, centre gave him the space and opportunity to show off his running skills, which took him through defences and past defenders all over the world.

A superb sense of anticipation and lightning pace were his strengths, but there were some who doubted his physical commitment and courage in defence as well as his ability to stand up to the rigours of international Rugby. Maso proved all his critics

wrong on the 1968 tour of New Zealand; in addition to his brilliant running, his involvement in all aspects of play was total. So much so that Colin Meads insisted that he would have Maso in his team 'at wing, centre, fly-half, name it. For the final Test at Auckland in 1968, they brought him into fly-half and we thought we could sew him up in close there. But he waltzed all around us. He would be in any world team of mine.'

Like many others, Meads appreciated Maso's fine sense of balance and poise in his deceptive running, allied with a delicate sense of timing in his passing. Yet, Maso was never really a regular in any French side, suffering from allegations of indiscipline, and was constantly out of favour with the selectors. Their policy was not one with which many Rugby supporters, anywhere, concurred and there were accusations that the team was picked by a 'forwards' mafia' who did not want the backs taking too much of the limelight. Those outside his country found his omissions strange. Chris Laidlaw said: 'Maso wafted in and out of French teams with the same apparent regularity with which he could, and perhaps still can, tear a midfield defence apart.' Maso won only seventeen international caps for France, scant reward for his undoubted talents.

Jo Maso, born in Toulouse in 1944, was the son of a Rugby League international and his father had a strong influence on his son's Rugby throughout his career. The youngster himself started off playing the thirteen-a-side game, but switched to Rugby Union before he was eighteen. The All Blacks, led by Whineray, provided his first real test when he played for the South-East Selection that met New Zealand in 1964. It was a hard game, with the visitors winning 8-5. Further promotion came when he played for France against Italy in the spring of 1966.

The five-foot-eleven and twelve-and-a-half-stone centre made his full international debut against Scotland in 1967. But it was not the debut he had hoped for; not only did France lose 9-8, but Maso twisted his ankle just before half-time and spent the rest of the game hobbling around at full-back. The centre, who was playing for Perpignan at the time, won two more caps in the Grand Slam year of 1968 and was selected to tour Australia and New Zealand that summer. The Test against the Wallabies and the final game against the All Blacks saw Maso at fly-half, where he proved an instant success and many critics thought that his future career might be at that position. In fact, he was to win only one more cap there, but the New Zealand supporters were already acclaiming him as the 'new Boniface' because of his beautiful style.

Maso switched clubs the following season, leaving Perpignan to go to Narbonne. But he was not granted the number one licence which is necessary to play in the club championship on the grounds that the club transfer appeared unjustifiable. So for a year Maso turned out for the Narbonne reserves. Luckily, he was not forgotten by the national selectors and was picked for the international against the Springboks at Bordeaux. Unfortunately, injury necessitated his withdrawal, but he proved his fitness with brilliant form for France against Romania. Maso won caps in the centre against Ireland and Scotland and appeared at fly-half to help deny Wales the Grand Slam with an 8-8 draw in Paris.

Again he suffered from injury and then selectorial inconsistencies, not appearing in any internationals until the Tests against South Africa in 1971 when he was injured and replaced by Dourthe during the second game. Amazingly, during his seven-year career for France, he never played one full season for his country. The centre was capped three times in 1972, scoring two tries in the 16-15 win over the Wallabies in Australia, and twice more in 1973.

Not many would have recognised his international career was over at this stage, but Jo Maso was never to play again for his country. There were many to back up his claims and Rugby enthusiasts everywhere could not understand why his name was always absent from French team-lists. There were various stories as to the reasons for his demise. Yet there was never any doubt about his footballing ability and it will always remain a source of mystery to Rugby fans all over the world why his country should have shunned the talents of Jo Maso; most countries, denied any midfield flair, would have been grateful to have such a rare and gifted player available.

Colin Meads

The finest forward produced by New Zealand and probably the outstanding Rugby personality of all time, Colin Meads dominated the world scene for over fifteen years and became the feared symbol of All Black strength and power. New Zealand scrum-half Chris Laidlaw, who played with Meads in many internationals, said: 'Colin Meads has given more to Rugby physically and spiritually than any other living player.' Willie John McBride, who was the New Zealander's great adversary on so many occasions, describes his opponent thus: 'Colin Meads was as hard a man as I ever have encountered. He was the best, most aggressive, and perhaps the most totally committed player I have ever opposed.'

Meads meant so much more to Rugby than his mere performances on the field; his very lifestyle as the New Zealand farmer who worked and trained with his brother Stan, also an All Black, and his unflinching dedication to New Zealand Rugby all helped to create the legend of the most famous name in Rugby. He first appeared for his country in 1957 and bowed out as captain after the 1971 series against the British Lions led by John Dawes.

Although some of his early Rugby was played at No. 8 and flanker, it was in the second row that he finally settled down, becoming one of the first of the new-breed 'tight-loose' forwards. Colin Meads with the ball in his hands, or more likely, hand, was a sight which thrilled crowds all over the world; he had fingers like sausages and his hand fitted like a claw around a Rugby ball. His runs were not restricted to charging, barging affairs; he could side-step and

Opposite *Colin Meads, in the colours of the RFU President's XV in 1971, won 55 caps for New Zealand in an international career that spanned 15 years.*
Below *Colin Meads, the legendary All Black forward, feeds the ball back to his scrum-half in one of his enormous hands.*

dummy with the best and there was a poise about his running which totally belied his six-foot-four, and sixteen-and-a-half-stone.

Meads set a style and standard for all future All Black forwards; not only did they have to be able to win the ball, but be able to use it and chase after it as well. Their duties were no longer restricted to playing a full part in the line-out, scrum, maul and ruck; now New Zealand forwards supported attacks, showing that fragile handling and primitive running by those in the 'boiler-room' was a thing of the past.

Every Rugby-playing country would have loved to have claimed Meads, although, perhaps along with South Africa, only New Zealand's environment would have brought out the best in 'Pinetree' as he was known everywhere. Coupled with his undoubted footballing talents, was a Rugby brain of a calibre few have been privileged to possess. To study Meads during a game was to watch one of the finest exponents of forward play—first there was the thorough fulfilment of his 'boiler-room' duties, then he excelled in the loose and dominated proceedings from start to finish, committing more than his fair share of defenders as they tried to stop this one-man Rugby machine.

Meads was also a deep thinker about the game and, after some early reservation, he changed his attitudes towards fifteen-man Rugby and became one of Freddie Allen's most influential disciples. The first decade of his international career had been spent permeating the legend of All Black forward play and ten-man Rugby. Allen came on the scene as coach and wanted to play a more expansive game. Meads was a big enough man to admit that Allen's philosophy was right and changed his own thinking on Rugby. Such was Meads' standing that his conversion greatly helped Allen's cause. Meads continued to spread the word even after he gave up playing; he now coaches King Country, the province with which his name will always be associated, and instils into his charges the idea of running Rugby.

Colin Earl Meads was born in Cambridge in Waikato in June 1936. He started playing Rugby in prep school at the age of eight and, by the time he was nineteen, had represented the King Country Schools, the senior provincial side and toured Australia and Ceylon with the New Zealand Under-23 team. An All Black trial followed in 1956 and the next year he won that All Black jersey that most of his life had been aimed at.

Those two Tests against the Australians were won and his year of triumph was completed when he scored a try in the second international. That try was the first of seven he scored for the All Blacks in fifty-five internationals, but it was the only one he scored from the wing position! Meads was deputising for the injured McMullen outside the centres, the ball came along the line and New Zealand's newest three-quarter hurled himself over in the corner. From that series until the end of 1971, Colin Meads was the most famous name in the New Zealand side. Some of those opening games were played in the middle of the back row or on the side of the scrum and it was a few years before he settled in the second row.

Meads was dropped for the opening Test against Ronnie Dawson's 1959 Lions, but reappeared as flanker for the next two and as No. 8 for the final Test. While not fixed in any one position, Meads was now an established and important member of the New Zealand pack. In the series against the South Africans in 1960, he appeared in the internationals at flanker, No. 8 and lock, playing some of his finest Rugby, the hard grounds suiting his hard-running style. He was much in demand, playing in twenty of the twenty-six games. If his potential and promise had been noted up to then, his performances on this tour earned him the respect of all opponents and their admiration as the best All Black forward. Yet, his uncompromising play and attitude was already causing grumblings and accusations of over-physical play that were to remain with him throughout his career.

Meads maintained his reputation as the world's best all-round forward in the 1961 home series against the French. In one of those internationals against France, Colin was joined in the All Blacks' pack by his younger brother Stan, who played on the flank. Stan Meads was an outstanding forward and is the player that Colin Meads would most like to have partner him in the second row, which he did many times in his career. Eventually, Stan decided to concentrate on his farming after the 1966 games against the British Lions and retired from international Rugby. (That first Test against the French saw three sets of brothers playing, the Meads and the Clarkes for New Zealand, and the Bonifaces on the opposing side.) Colin was dropped for the second and final time in his international career after the 1962 9-9 draw against the Wallabies at Wellington; he was in good company – also out were Dennis Young, Kel Tremain and

Colin Meads in his ninetieth game for the All Blacks, against the North of England on Brian Lochore's 1967 tour.

Ian Clarke. Ironically, it was Stan who replaced his brother in the second row.

In the next game the Meads brothers were together in the New Zealand second row for the first time and 'Pinetree' was never again to feel the axe of the All Black selectors. Meads enhanced his reputation on Whineray's tour of Great Britain and France and the visit also brought him into contact with the Irish lock who is as respected as Meads is in Rugby circles, Willie John McBride. The pair quickly established their physical commitment in the Ireland-New Zealand international, whence they enjoyed a rivalry and healthy respect unparalleled in modern Rugby. Ireland were unlucky to lose that game, but generally it was a very successful tour for the All

Blacks, with Colin Meads featuring strongly as one of the dominating personalities.

The All Blacks' pack of the sixties was now at its peak with Colin Meads, more than any other single player, symbolising its strength, power, ruthlessness, commitment and skill. A New Zealand side without Meads at this time would have been like playing cricket without the bails or tennis without the net. His mere presence seemed to intimidate the opposition and the Springboks of 1965 and the British Lions of 1966 were seen off with little trouble.

There were those who suggested that Meads might be losing some of his stamina and strength when he was selected to tour Britain under Brian Lochore in 1967 at the age of thirty-one. These doubts were quickly dispelled and Meads was once again 'king-pin' of the New Zealand forwards. It was on this tour that he suffered what many thought was inevitable because of his over-energetic physical play: he was sent off. Meads, who had already been officially cautioned, was sent off two minutes from the end of the Scotland-New Zealand international at Murrayfield on December 2, 1967 by referee Kevin Kelleher of Ireland.

The bare facts are that Meads broke from a ruck in pursuit of the ball and lunged with his boot as the Scottish fly-half picked the ball up. Referee Kelleher said: 'In my view, Meads was indifferent as to whether he kicked the ball or the player.' Meads was suspended for the next two games, but his sentence was over long before the controversy on the rights and wrongs of the incident had subsided. The irony of the situation was that Colin Meads was sent off for one of the lesser incidents of the many in which he was involved during his career. Meads maintains: 'I repeat, I have never deliberately kicked or attempted to kick any man.' The New Zealand lock was very worried about being remembered, first and foremost, as only the second All Black, after Cyril Brownlie, to be sent off, but such is the measure of his playing achievements

that this has not nor ever would have happened. Other controversies concerning Meads involved injuries to Clive Rowlands, Jeff Young, David Watkins, and Wallaby scrum-half Ken Catchpole, whose career was ended when Meads tried to pull him out of a ruck in an international in 1968. There was never any doubt about Mead's commitment when he pulled on an All Black jersey, but perhaps this commitment carried him over the top and it is worth noting that Meads was rarely on the receiving end of these exchanges. Yet few who played against him would accuse him of being dirty and, as his style was abrasive and geared towards physical contact and contest, it is not surprising that he often found himself in trouble.

It is ironic that the sending-off should happen in the year when Meads finally accepted Freddie 'The Needle' Allen's attacking principles. Allen was renowned for his psychological attack on players and had once described Meads as a 'doddering old bugger, who played forty minutes as a lock and the rest as a scavenging side-row forward.' Chris Laidlaw recalls another incident when Meads suffered from Allen's tongue: 'Nobody messed around when "The Needle" gave them a team talk. Once, for instance, shortly before a vital Test match and in the middle of an Allen monologue, Colin Meads let slip a nervous yawn. 'Am I boring you, Colin?' said Allen in a taut voice. Meads went out and played with the fear of the devil in him. If Allen had Meads so much in his pocket, it is not difficult to imagine his effect on the lesser souls of the team.'

Allen insisted that the ball was won principally to give to the backs. Some of the New Zealand forwards who had been used to running the show were slow to accept the new style, but once 'Pinetree' had been converted, the battle was over and the All Blacks emerged to play some of their finest Rugby on this tour. There was no sign that the veteran 'war-horse' was slowing up and, as usual, he was at the core of the New Zealand wins over France in 1968 and Wales in 1969.

It looked as if Colin Meads would reach his peak on the 1970 tour of South Africa, which also saw him as vice-captain to Brian Lochore. Right from the start Meads was in top form, and Meads in top form was so much better than anyone else. But he had his arm broken in the match against Eastern Transvaal in the sixth game of the tour. The lock was desperately disappointed because he knew it was going to be his final opportunity of putting one over on the Springboks. Fit again, he recovered to play in the final two Tests, but by then the series was lost. Of his fifty-five internationals for New Zealand, forty-one were won and only ten lost. After the 1960 series against South Africa, the All Blacks had lost only two of the next thirty-eight games, until that 1970 battle against South Africa.

Yet in his final six caps, he was only on the winning side once, taking part in two losing series. After that South African defeat, Meads returned to lead the All Blacks against John Dawes' Lions in 1971, but the great pack of the sixties had broken up and New Zealand was going through a transitional period; even Brian Lochore was brought out of retirement to partner Meads in the second row for the third Test. However, Meads was unable to inspire the All Blacks to victory and the series was lost 2-1. Meads was as magnanimous in defeat as he was modest and gracious in victory. He appreciated that British forward play had grown up and no longer allowed itself to be intimidated.

Later that year Colin Meads suffered terrible injuries in a car accident and his back had to be put in plaster. Yet, within six months he was back playing Rugby; the giant of Rugby was seemingly indestructible. But Meads had decided that his All Blacks' days were over. The New Zealanders knew they would miss him once he had gone, but it was not until he had retired that they found out just how much. It was not only his presence on the field, but his influence on the younger players and colleagues to whom 'Pinetree' was almost something sacred and whose word was treated as law. Some of those words of wisdom could have been used on Ian Kirkpatrick's 1972-73 tour; and it was not only the younger players who seemed to have needed parental control.

Luckily his influence is still felt at his beloved Waitete club and in King Country. When the Lions visited there in 1977, it was the first time since 1950 there was no Meads in the side to play them, but his role as coach meant his presence was still felt by the British side. It was never likely that Colin Meads would be lost to Rugby, or Rugby lost to Meads. They are part of one another, interwoven so closely that it is impossible to see where one ends and the other begins; it is simpler to say that they both need each other to have survived as they have done.

Bryn Meredith

The Newport hooker who dominated the Welsh national side for nigh on a decade and was an important figure on three British Lions' tours, Bryn Meredith was also one of the outstanding Rugby personalities of the past quarter of a century. He was the perfect gentleman and diplomat whose skills and talent were matched by his attitude to team-mate and opponent alike. The complete master of his trade, Meredith is probably the finest hooker to have graced a Rugby field since the last war. Meredith was not only a fine hooker, but also a fine forward whose speed around the field was truly amazing. And this pace, coupled with secure hands and good positioning, brought him many tries at club and international level. These qualities can be judged by the fact that he was a top-class sevens player.

No matter the level of game or where it was played, Meredith gave his all and was a

Bryn Meredith, in his final season for Wales, kicks upfield in the game against France at Cardiff, which Wales won 3-0.

model of consistency. He set standards of play and behaviour that his team-mates strove to attain and their respect for him made him an excellent choice as captain; he led Newport and Wales with distinction. Wherever Meredith played or toured, he was held in esteem for his performances and scrupulous attitude on the field and for his friendly, helpful behaviour off it. Even when things were not going the way he had hoped, as on the 1959 Lions' tour when he was second choice behind skipper Ronnie Dawson, his loyalty was unquestioned and all his energy was geared towards the good of the team. Meredith was a player who

reached the top yet never compromised his beliefs or the spirit in which the game of Rugby football is meant to be played. There can be no better example for any aspiring newcomer to follow.

Meredith ruled unchallenged in the Welsh side for thirty-four caps, beginning in 1954, and played on three consecutive Lions' tours. He established himself as world-class and it says a lot for his dedication that he remained at the top for the next seven years. His dedication to the Newport club and the cause of Welsh and Lions' Rugby was always tempered with a belief in the spirit of Rugby football.

Born in Pontnewydd in 1932, Brinley Victor Meredith learnt his Rugby at West Monmouth Grammar School, later to produce one-third of the Pontypool front-row,

116

Bryn Meredith in aggressive action against the Springboks; he played in all eight Tests against South Africa on the 1955 and 1962 Lions' tours.

against Ireland in 1954 and was to remain a fixture until his retirement in 1962, missing only two matches – one for a family bereavement and one when dropped in 1959.

Meredith was chosen for the 1955 Lions' tour to South Africa and it provided a perfect opportunity for him to show off his technical and running skills. First choice for the four Tests, the Springbok players and crowd soon learned to respect this talented Welsh hooker. The Lions' front-row of Courtenay Meredith, Bryn Meredith and Bill Williams is rated by the Newport hooker as the finest unit he ever played in during his long career. His hooking duels with van der Merwe in the Test series were absorbing and when Meredith returned home, he left behind a reputation as one of the finest hookers ever to have visited South Africa.

Wales won the championship the season after his return and yet, while the Newport player consolidated his position as the world's best, the choice of Ronnie Dawson as skipper of the Lions' party to New Zealand meant only a number two spot for Meredith. Dawson, of course, was Ireland's hooker, but many thought that the Welshman's class would mean he would force his way into the Test side. In the Australian part of the tour, to supply a need, Meredith played on the flank; but on the concrete ground, he suffered a very bad hamstring injury and it was well into the New Zealand stage of the tour before he was back to his old self again. In the meantime, Meredith was 'President of the Social Club' and playing as full a part as he could in the welfare of the tourists and their hosts.

But by the time of the fourth and final Test, Meredith was pressing hard for a spot in the team. Meredith was probably in better form than his skipper, but to retain continuity, Dawson was in the middle of the front row when the team was selected. Meredith accepted the decision in the only way he knew how – with dignity, ready to support his team, although he was on the

Graham Price. In 1949 Meredith was selected for the Welsh Secondary Schools; with him in that side was a fly-half who later toured South Africa with Meredith, Cliff Morgan. After leaving school, he joined the Royal Navy as part of his national service, and there played for Devonport Services, the Royal Navy, Devon and, when home on leave, Newport. He played twice against Bob Stuart's All Blacks, at hooker for Devon and at prop for Newport. These displays plus his performances for St Luke's College, where he was now studying, brought him in line for a Welsh cap when Dai Davies retired. Meredith made his debut

side-lines. He more than anyone was pleased when the Lions emerged 9-6 victors.

However, there were plenty of honours left for Meredith, with the 1961-62 season being one of his most successful and satisfying. He skippered the Newport side that not only won the Welsh club championship, but also the 'Snelling Sevens'. He led the Welsh side to its first win over France for five years and was then selected for his third Lions' tour in succession. And to cap it all, Meredith was voted 'Sports Personality of the Year' in Wales, an honour which he appreciated very much. He regained his Test place in South Africa, playing in all four Tests. He devoted himself to the party's well-being as he had done in the two tours before, now very much the elder statesman and a valuable counsellor to the younger players.

He aired a desire to retire from both club and international commitments when he came back from South Africa. Newport had injuries, so he was soon back playing at prop. His final international was the postponed game against Ireland; his opponent, ironically, that same Ronnie Dawson and they battled hard as did the sides in a three-all draw. Meredith had had enough and afterwards announced his retirement from first-class Rugby. It had been a notable career and he had dominated the Rugby scene as a player and a personality for almost a decade. Wales have had many excellent hookers since the last war – Dai Davies, Bryn Meredith, Norman Gale, Jeff Young and Bobby Windsor. No country has been better served, with Bryn Meredith the finest of a very exceptional bunch.

Lucien Mias

The attitude and Rugby brain of French second-row forward Lucien Mias managed to unite eight unpredictable forwards to work for the benefit of their country's

Lucien Mias, France's captain and inspiration on their 1958 tour to South Africa, where they beat the Springboks in the Test series.

Rugby. France has always had outstanding leaders and Mias' task in harnessing the Latin temperament for the cause was no less formidable than Napoleon's. Through Mias, French forwards found a reason for existence and they responded by beating the best in the world.

Mias had been a member of the French pack that had been ground into nothing by Basil Kenyon's Springboks in 1952 and left for dead, 25-3. Unlike the majority of his colleagues, Mias took exception to this humiliation. Six years later, under Mias' guidance, France came and conquered. This victory was all the more satisfying because Mias had spent four years away from the international arena as a result of his medical studies. It was a remarkable resurrection and his place in French Rugby history is assured for ever. Without him, French forwards might have wandered for ever in search of dreams. Thanks to Mias, they are now all searching for roughly the same vision of ultimate Rugby. Mias, more than anyone else, is the reason for this unity; he gave French Rugby the direction which allowed its undoubted skill to find acceptance in world terms; without that direction, their Rugby would have taken much longer to grow up.

It was that 1952 Springbok defeat which motivated Mias' quest; his shame was complete as French forward power was eclipsed by South Africa. What annoyed Mias even more was the way his countrymen accepted this disaster lightly. The two most important years in his Rugby career were 1952 and 1958, both occasions of French-Springbok Rugby battles; it was the excitable and volatile against the cool and calculating.

Mias knew that the French had the ability; it was his task to unite the players and raise their game. His charges were talented but unruly, yet Mias was successful

in motivating France's finest to their heart's work and his job was completed with great personal satisfaction. Having shown the way, Mias returned for one more season before retiring. He had given French Rugby a gentle push in the direction which it should have been following for years.

Lucien Mias, who was born at Saint-Germain-de-Calberte (Lozère), came into the French side at the age of twenty. His style was similar to his colleagues in the pack at that time–spontaneous, attractive, but undisciplined and lacking in tactical appreciation. The forwards were a poor second to the outstanding French running backs. Mias remained a regular in the national

Lucien Mias is chaired off the field by his side after they had beaten Wales 11-3 at Colombes in 1959, a championship year for France.

team for the next four seasons, beginning in 1951, and won fifteen caps before switching his career from schoolteaching to medicine. Those medical studies required his withdrawal from the international scene.

But that 1952 Springbok defeat was still in his thoughts and he continued playing for his club, Mazamet. His approach changed with the realisation of the vital importance of set play, especially the scrum. His game had gained vision and he transformed himself and the Mazamet side into a team where the forwards worked as a unit, not eight individuals. Mias's dedication to the cause was such that he also lost three stone in an effort to make himself more suited to the new style of Rugby.

France did not manage to score a single point in the 1957 International Championship. Mias was then persuaded that his style

and approach were necessary to restore his country's flagging Rugby fortunes. And Lucien Mias saw his opportunity for revenge when asked to lead France to South Africa in the summer of 1958.

Some critics thought that his slimming down and new style had taken the edge off his aggressive approach, but he proved them all wrong on that tour. For the first time this century, the Springboks lost a home series. French pride was restored with a 3-3 draw in the first Test and the historic 9-5 victory in the second, before which Mias is reputed to have drunk half a bottle of rum. That is as maybe, but his philosophy had been proved correct and French sides have tried to balance their passionate, unpredictable nature with tactical appreciation ever since. It was an international championship year for France in 1959, after which Mias departed from the scene once more, having shown his country the way. They may have strayed occasionally since then, but France have generally followed the general direction pointed out by Lucien Mias over twenty years ago.

Cliff Morgan

Cliff Morgan was the guiding light of Welsh and British Lions' sides in the mid-fifties. His romantic image of the game remained untarnished even after the pressure of several years at the highest level; his enthusiasm was complete and his love for Rugby remains as pure today as when he first learnt the game in the Rhondda. On and off the field, Cliff Morgan is one of the finest ambassadors ever produced by Rugby or any other sport—he has an unflinching belief in the spirit of the game and in its value to the individual. As a player, he was a fly-half of typical Welsh talent, coupling his natural ability with a tactical awareness of genius as he learnt all the game had to offer.

Short, dark and sturdy, Cliff Isaac

Morgan was from the mould of the traditional outside half. He stood five foot seven and weighed twelve stone in his playing days. His speed over the first few yards, which took him through defences and past flankers all over the world, was his outstanding quality. He would swerve away in an arc from the defence off the scrum and straighten up, leaving players trailing in his wake, unable to cope with his electric pace. And it was on the hard grounds of South Africa, rather than the soft-going at home, that he proved his qualities of genius. By the time of that tour with the Lions in 1955, he had grasped the importance of tactical kicking, leaving early memories of

Many thought Wales would have difficulty replacing a player of Cliff Morgan's calibre at fly-half, but David Watkins, Barry John and Phil Bennett have helped ease the worries.

inadequacies in that department lost in the hazy heat of South Africa. In defence, Morgan seemed like another member of the back row as he repeatedly appeared to save his side with a tackle or clearing kick.

His contribution to any side was never restricted to those eighty minutes on the park. Always the outstanding personality, Cliff Morgan possessed unbounded energy and would generally be found at the centre of most activities – telling jokes, leading the singing, playing the piano and keeping the morale of his colleagues as high as possible; invaluable qualities, especially when players are away from home for months at a time.

Born in Trebanog in the Rhondda Valley in 1930, his promise of future achievements had shown itself at school. Morgan would have appeared for the Welsh Secondary side sooner than he did had he not missed a season and a half with pleurisy, caught

Cliff Morgan for once is caught by a Springbok on the 1955 Lions' tour of South Africa, but this was a rare occurrence.

because he was replaced in a schools' trial and had to sit around in his wet jersey as there were no clean ones available. It meant a wait until the 1948-49 season before regaining his place. Later that year Morgan took his considerable talents to Cardiff, making the first-team fly-half spot his own when Billy Cleaver retired after the 1950 Lions' tour to New Zealand. His scrum-half partner at the club was Rex Willis and they were together when Morgan made his debut for Wales against Ireland at the Arms Park in 1951. The match was drawn 3-3, the other debutant that day, Ben Edwards, kicking the penalty goal that levelled the scores. For Morgan it was the start of a distinguished career; for Edwards, a first and last cap.

Basil Kenyon's Springboks were the fly-half's opponents in his third international. Morgan had impressed the South Africans in their club game against Cardiff; the visitors had won, but only narrowly, and looked upon this young player as a great danger in the forthcoming international. The Springboks decided to use their back row – van Wyk, Muller and Fry – to pressure Morgan and try and box him in; the tactic worked. With the back row hounding him all the game, the youngster panicked, kicked hurriedly and badly; the South African objective had been achieved. His performance can be best summed up by saying that had Wales had the Cliff Morgan of a few seasons later, they would certainly have won that day.

But that was one of Wales' few setbacks that season. With Morgan learning his lessons from the Springbok defeat and recovering his confidence quickly, it was a Grand Slam, Triple Crown and Championship year for the Principality. And when Bob Stuart's All Blacks appeared in 1953, Morgan was at the heart of two historic victories – for Cardiff and for Wales; over twenty-five years later, both sides are still waiting to repeat the event. Cliff Morgan had proved himself a world-class player;

the only blemish on an inspiring career was that Springbok defeat. The 1955 Lions' tour to South Africa provided the ideal opportunity to erase that memory. So well did he play on that tour, so perfectly tuned were his numerous talents, that he is regarded by many as the greatest fly-half ever to visit there. The perfect conditions, the hard grounds, one of the finest British backlines of all times and Morgan's genius all combined for the exhibition of the player's finest Rugby.

The boxing-in tactic by South African forwards was tried time and time again, but he became the scourge of back rows everywhere, evading the loose-forward screen with an apparent ease which did not always make Cliff Morgan a great favourite with Springbok forwards. But the crowds loved him; not only for his own creativity, but for

Whether with the ball in his hands or at his feet, Cliff Morgan was one of the finest post-war fly-halves.

his ability in bringing out the best in his backs, who included Butterfield, Davies, Pedlow and O'Reilly. His partnership with Jeff Butterfield was something special and as a pair they complemented each other perfectly.

That Morgan had completely recovered from that 1951 game was evident by the try he scored in the first Test at Ellis Park, described by many as the 'greatest game of all time', when the Lions emerged 23-22 winners. Apart from Daan Retief replacing Muller, the Springbok back row was the same as four years previously, as was the proposed way to deal with the fly-half menace. But Morgan had learnt well and did not allow the trio of loose forwards to intimidate him. In the opening minutes of the second-half, Morgan proved his control was complete. Receiving a long pass from Dickie Jeeps, after the Lions had won a scrum on the right-hand side of the field, Morgan's electrifying pace took him through the back-row cover and across the Springbok 25-yard line. As he straightened on the arc which had taken him past the defence and with van Wyk trailing behind, Morgan sprinted to score one of Rugby's most memorable tries. His Rugby education was complete; his mature judgement now ensured that his many skills were utilised to the maximum.

Later that tour, he led the Lions to victory in the third Test at Pretoria when tour leader Ronnie Thompson was injured. It is an occasion that Morgan declares was his proudest moment in Rugby. The Test series was eventually drawn 2-2, but the tour was a personal triumph for Morgan; he had been the outstanding personality and was the focal point of some of the best running-Rugby ever played by a British side.

Morgan returned to play in the International Championship for three seasons, Wales winning the title in 1956, before retiring with a record 29 caps for a Welsh fly-half. This is a record recently equalled by Phil Bennett and their careers and style have much in common; both played their best Rugby in South Africa, both were very quick off the mark at the start of a run and both were cover tacklers of uncanny anticipation. While Cliff Morgan was a fixture in the Welsh side for those seven years, an injury before the game against Australia in 1957 gave the selectors a chance to bring in a fly-half who would have certainly played many times for his country had Morgan not been around; the fly-half's name – Carwyn James, who was later to win a second cap, outside Morgan, in the centre against France in 1958 and who provided the coaching inspiration for the British Lions in New Zealand in 1971.

Cliff Morgan decided to call it a day when he felt that he had lost some of the speed that had cut numerous holes in numerous defences. But he was not lost to the game and has kept in touch as a writer, commentator and more recently as head of the BBC's outside broadcasts. Cliff Morgan loves the game and loved playing the game; this was obvious to all who watched him. It was part of his charm, a charm that has infatuated people all over the world; his contribution to the game, whether for Wales, Cardiff, the Barbarians or the Lions, will always be measured in much more than just his performances on the field.

Graham Mourie

Graham Mourie is still a relative newcomer to the international scene; he made his New Zealand debut in the third Test against Phil Bennett's Lions in 1977. Yet, already, he has created an enormous impact, both as a world-class flanker, and as an All Black captain to rank with the likes of Wilson Whineray and Brian Lochore. And in just over a year as skipper, Graham Mourie's name was written large in the record books as the first New Zealand captain to achieve the Grand Slam in Britain – victories over Ireland, Wales, England and Scotland; Mourie's control, influence and individual performance were a major factor in that success.

When Mourie was picked to lead the Eighth All Blacks, he was the third consecutive back-row forward to take New Zealand to Britain (the fourth if you include Andy Leslie's 1974 visit as part of Ireland's centenary celebrations). Yet, even in these days of instant communication, Mourie was very much an unknown quantity with the British public when the party arrived in October 1978. When they left, two months later, the general opinion was that not only was Graham Mourie a superb flanker, but a captain who commanded a rare loyalty and response from his players. Always helpful and polite, he formed an effective and popular management trio with Russ Thomas and coach Jack Gleeson.

The British tour was the third time that Jack Gleeson had toured with Mourie as his captain. It seemed a partnership destined to lead All Black Rugby into the eighties, but illness meant Gleason had to give up the post of coach in 1979; it was a tragic blow to New Zealand Rugby.

Mourie, like Gleeson, wanted to play 15-man Rugby. Perhaps that was a throwback to the flanker's early days. Born in Opunake in 1952, his early career was spent at fly-half, where he represented the Under-12 provincial side. Later, he toured Australia as a lock with the Taranaki Secondary Schools side in 1969. By the seventies, however, Mourie decided—against the advice of his father who considered his son too slow—to move to the side of the scrum.

Those early days saw Graham Neil Kenneth Mourie advance up the traditional All Black ladder of recognition—New Zealand Colts (1972); NZ Juniors and NZ Universities (1973). And also in 1973 he made his provincial debut for Wellington, scoring a try in their 25-16 defeat of the visiting England side.

By now, full international honours were beckoning. Yet, although he gave a good performance in the trials, Mourie's name was not among those chosen for the visit to Ireland in 1974. His university career finished the following year and he returned to Taranaki to join his brother on the farm.

All Black flanker Graham Mourie, an outstanding leader of the 1978 and 1979 New Zealanders on and off the field.

Graham Mourie, the popular captain on the 1978 All Blacks, which became the first New Zealand side to achieve the Grand Slam in Britain.

Mourie was given the captaincy of the NZ Juniors on an internal tour and he seemed a certainty for the full tour to South Africa in 1976, but a rib-cartilage injury ended his hopes of even making the trials.

However, there was consolation when he was chosen to lead a party of 25 All Blacks to Argentina while the top players were still battling the Springboks. With Mourie at No. 8, both Tests were won convincingly and the new skipper proved himself a popular and successful leader. It was on this trip that he got to really know Jack Gleeson and vice versa. Gleeson had found the captain he wanted to lead New Zealand into a more expansive game. The coach recalled later: 'I came back to New Zealand at the end of the Argentinian tour and said, there and then, that Mourie would be one of the great New Zealand captains. Mourie and I have both the same views on Rugby, our likings for the game are the same. We get on well together and, of course, this is instilled into the team. There are no conflicts.'

Yet the Taranaki flanker was missing from the All Black side to play Bennett's 1977 Lions in the first Test—a poor trial had seen to that—and he had to wait until the third game before making his international debut. It was a New Zealand side that contained six changes—another notable inclusion that day was Bevan Wilson who made a dream start at full-back. The third and fourth Tests went the All Blacks' way, the series was won and New Zealand had found themselves a new flanker. And when the side was chosen to tour France in late 1977, New Zealand had found a new captain, Graham Mourie. It was a successful visit—a lot of new All Black talent emerged and New Zealand out-ran and out-played France to win the second Test and square the series.

Mourie missed the 1978 home series against Australia because of injury and lock Frank Oliver took over, but the captaincy reverted to the flanker when the party to tour Britain was nominated. Mourie said at the start of that tour: 'Although history has shown that it is the results of the Test matches that count, I would like us to be judged for our performances on and off the field and for the type of Rugby we play.'

Although their back play lost its sparkle after a promising start and the penultimate game against Bridgend left an ugly taste, the eighth All Blacks will be remembered as a friendly and well-behaved bunch and the first New Zealand side to gain the Grand Slam. The captain, Graham Mourie, can take a lot of credit for the plus marks on that tour.

His speed around the park was breath-taking; if you were watching the All Blacks and he was not the first to the breakdown, then he probably wasn't playing that afternoon. His tackling was engulfing and totally effective and he saved his side many times by appearing in the right place at the right time in defence. If his backs needed support, he was there; if the loose ball needed tidying up, then Mourie was there again. His work-rate seemed almost suicidal, yet he still found time to cajole his players and keep them going for the whole game. They responded by never giving up—a factor which proved conclusive in many games. He led the All Blacks to Test victories in Scotland and England in 1979.

Graham Mourie has achieved so much so soon in his career, and has set himself standards that will be hard to follow. But Mourie, more than most, has the character and ability to keep on top.

Tony O'Reilly

Ireland's wonder wing Tony O'Reilly achieved world Rugby fame before he was nineteen. A player with freckles and film-star looks coupled with the almost customary Irish 'gift of the gab', it says much for his mature attitude that he was able to cope with the adulation and hero-worship he received on his two Lions' tours, while still remaining a firm favourite with his team-mates. There are many, even much older, who would have allowed their heads to have been turned away from the Rugby field towards the bright lights. O'Reilly's attraction was further enhanced by his 'devilish' treatment of those in authority, especially amongst the players who would have loved to have treated the 'bosses' with such humorous disdain. O'Reilly believed totally in Rugby as a game to be enjoyed and he lost patience with those who tried to make it otherwise.

That 1955 tour to South Africa established Tony O'Reilly as one of the great characters in Rugby and his company was eagerly sought by those who wanted to listen to the Irish raconteur whose anecdotes were sprinkled with marvellous accents and mimicry. But behind all this, there was, and still is, a very devoted and serious Irishman,

Tony O'Reilly barges over for his record-breaking seventeenth try, in the fourth Test against the All Blacks in 1959.

sensitive to his country's and countrymen's needs; in many ways, very much the patriot.

O'Reilly was always striking in appearance. A huge frame – six-foot-two and fifteen stone – adorned with auburn hair and boyish good looks with legs that would normally be encased in shorts seemingly two sizes too small and offering great quantities of thigh for view . . . very much the resurrection of the Greek and Roman gods and, in many cases, treated in the same

reverent way. Like many before and since, he played his best Rugby on tour. In Irish sides, Tony O'Reilly was outstanding without too much effort or training; and he was a player whose weight rose dramatically if not in trim. But on tour there was no escape and usually by the end of three hard months of training and playing, O'Reilly was the perfect athlete and in superb form. The five/six month gap between the end of a tour and the beginning of Ireland's bid on the International Championship was certainly not beneficial in O'Reilly's case.

This would partly explain why he scored sixteen tries in South Africa in 1955, seventeen in New Zealand in 1959 and only five in twenty-nine appearances for his country in a career that spanned from 1955 to 1963 (with a surprise recall in 1970). The other reason, undoubtedly, was the quality of talent around him. The Lions' sides of 1955 and 1959 were exceptionally well served in the backs. In South Africa, there were Jeeps, Morgan, Davies and Butterfield to put him away and in 1959 he was fed by Jeeps, Risman, Scotland, Price and Hewitt. The Irish backs were good, but not that good. And as O'Reilly could never be described as a busy player, if the ball was not reaching him he was unlikely to go looking for it. It is strange that in his beloved Ireland, he is regarded less as a world-class wing (as he is in South Africa and New Zealand) and more as a Rugby character, who has since become one of the most successful businessmen in the world. But a measure of his Rugby skill can be judged from the inscription on a shield presented to O'Reilly by his school, Belvedere College: 'To Tony O'Reilly who in the first year after leaving school was selected for Leinster, Ireland, the Barbarians and the British Lions.'

And Anthony John Francis O'Reilly, born in 1937, had been an oustanding athlete at school, excelling at cricket, tennis and soccer as well as Rugby. There is an unwritten law in Irish Rugby circles that even the most promising newcomer must serve his apprenticeship in the junior sides. But, O'Reilly was too good to be held back and, with a disregard for the norm that was to become a hallmark of O'Reilly in later days, he was selected for the final Irish trial less than a month after making his senior club debut. That was January 1955 and three months later he had played four times for his country and was picked as a member of the 1955 British Lions. It had not been a successful year for Ireland – three defeats and a draw – but young O'Reilly, playing in the centre, had shown enough potential.

The quality of the Lions' centres meant a

move for the young Irishman to the wing; he did not worry – there was probably more chance of getting the ball there with the Lions than in the centre for Ireland. His weight and speed brought him many tries and his looks many admirers. But he showed maturity well beyond his years, coped easily with the pressures and impressed his elder colleagues with his quiet, intelligent attitude.

In fact, everyone was impressed with the youngster whose performances on and off the field made him one of the personalities of the tour. O'Reilly travelled the world for the following three summers; Canada (1957) and South Africa (1958) with the Barbarians and New Zealand (1959) with Ronnie Dawson's Lions.

He was not always held in the same aura back in Ireland as he was abroad. A shoulder dislocation in the final Test in South Africa in 1955 had left the wing slightly susceptible to injury and there were accusations that his devotion to Irish club Rugby was not all it should be, especially when he moved to England and played for Leicester. This intelligent Irishman had graduated as a solicitor before attaining a degree in civil law. His business took him to Leicester before returning to Dublin. (He has achieved as much, if not more, in the business world as he did on the Rugby field; O'Reilly is one of the highest-paid men in his field and is very much the jet-travelling tycoon. To O'Reilly, Rugby was a sport, a pastime; his career as a businessman would receive all his hard work and devotion.)

The next highlight of his career was the 1959 Lions' tour to New Zealand. And, although O'Reilly won his final cap in 1970, this series against the All Blacks was his last real success. If he had been king in South Africa in 1955, then he was god in 1959. Admired by all, he was the tour's number one pin-up and responded by playing some of his finest running Rugby and scoring many spectacular tries. One of the best was his effort in the final Test when he scored his

Tony O'Reilly, the pin-up boy of Irish and Lions' Rugby in the fifties who has now found great success in the business world.

seventeenth to set a new record for a Lion in New Zealand. O'Reilly had received the pass for that final try from the replacement scrum-half on the tour, Ireland's Andy Mulligan. His arrival meant the creation of one of Rugby's best-known and funniest double acts–O'Reilly and Mulligan. The pair mimicked all around, being good enough for their repertoire to be broadcast on NZ radio.

O'Reilly returned home with his reputation never higher, but his run of twenty-two consecutive Irish caps was soon interrupted by injury and then the whims of the national selectors. His career total of caps seemed destined to be twenty-eight when he was left out after 1963, but, amazingly, Tony O'Reilly was recalled for the 1970 game

against England at Twickenham to take his total to twenty-nine appearances for Ireland.

In contrast with his career with the Lions, the wing was only on the winning side ten times with Ireland and scored only five tries, a famine ration for one so talented. While O'Reilly was around, Ireland never won the championship or more than two games in any international season.

But despite coming off the field a victor in only one of his eight outings against England, O'Reilly is very fond of the English and their ways and this profile would not be complete without one of his many anecdotes.

'It is often said that England start five points up at Twickenham. Stephen Potter would delight at the many ploys devised to reduce this handicap–like the misshapen Irish front-row forward breaking into the dressing room when Eric Evans, wearing a red nose and a matching face, was giving a final harangue to the English team: "Remember our history! Waterloo!" (with an Irish captain), "Alamein!" (with another one). "Order and discipline will defeat Irish individualism," he said. "Excuse me, lads," interrupted a friendly Irish face, "but has anyone got any hairy twine for me boots?"'

Frik du Preez

Forward Frik du Preez eventually settled in the second row where he proved himself one of the fastest locks ever to play international Rugby. His pace coupled with one of the best jumping techniques pushed this Springbok to the forefront of world Rugby for over a decade. Colin Meads went so far as to rate him the quickest lock who ever played Rugby: 'Locks vary a lot. Frik was never a head-down worker. He had a terrific sense for getting to where the ball was and running hard. He was a chaser and an individual.' And it was this speed around the park that first brought him to promin-

South African lock Frik Du Preez demonstrates the jumping ability that made him such a dominating force in world Rugby in the sixties.

were ideally suited to the charging runs of this forward, though it was noticeable that in soft conditions – Britain and New Zealand – it sometimes took the lock time to get under way. Yet even without this attribute Frederick Christoffel Hendrick du Preez would have still been a fixture in the South African side. His line-out jumping was of such a high standard that it consistently provided secure possession wherever the Springboks were playing.

Not that du Preez was that tall—he stood six foot two—but his perfect timing in take-off brought him to his maximum jumping height just when the ball was overhead and he was able to beat opponents who were inches taller. His early international days were spent on the flank and, perhaps because of this, he never earned the reputation of being a powerful scrummager as he was usually more intent on breaking away in order to become involved in the loose play.

Du Preez loved the unorthodox: during his career he scored some marvellous tries, some from far distances for a supposedly tight forward. This Springbok was a fine footballer whose movement contained a certain grace and poise which seemed in direct competition with his bulk. His unorthodoxy stretched even far enough for him to have been a goal-kicker in his early international days, kicking two penalty goals in the Springboks' 12-5 win over Scotland on Malan's 1960-61 tour. And he showed his versatility to perfection in a Currie Cup game for Northern Transvaal. He followed up a thirty-yard run for a try with a fifty-yard penalty before finally dropping a sixty-five yard goal. Not bad for a lock, a position not normally associated with such scoring feats.

The future Springbok forward was born in 1936 and educated at Rustenburg high school. First notice of him came during the 1960 All Blacks' tour of South Africa; although he did not play in any of the internationals, the New Zealand visitors were impressed with his play, especially his line-out technique. And this form won him a place in Avril Malan's party that came to Britain in 1960-61. As yet it was undecided whether he was better suited to play at lock or on the flank, but it was in the latter position that du Preez made his initial

impression. It was a successful tour for him, playing in sixteen matches including the Test wins against England and Scotland on the flank, and he was the second highest scorer with fifty-eight points behind Dick Lockyear. The team he entered was a powerful combination and he had to wait until the 1964 game against France before suffering a reversal in a Springbok jersey.

By that time, du Preez's ability had become known to the Wallabies and the 1962 British Lions as well as the Welsh side that toured South Africa in 1964. It was still as a flanker that du Preez was selected, giving him a chance to show his devastating form in the loose. During the tour of Australasia, the forward made the move to the second row of the scrum and his displays there brought high praise from the New Zealand critics and it was noticeable that local sides varied their line-out tactics when du Preez was playing against them. He ruled the roost in the jumping department and played in the six internationals, five of which were lost.

The lock was missing from most of the series against France, but returned for the fourth Test when again he controlled the line-out. Re-established in the side, du Preez was in magnificent form against the 1968 British Lions, scoring one of the finest individual tries ever seen in South Africa. During the first Test, the lock peeled from a line-out and ran fifty yards to score with the British side unable to stop him. He had been a dominant figure in both the 1962 and 1968 internationals against the Lions and he was held in high esteem by British players. Unfortunately, he did not show his best form on de Villiers' 1969-70 tour of Britain where the soft, wet conditions did not suit his style, although he was still a force to be reckoned with in the line-out.

Happy again on the hard grounds of his own country, du Preez was in excellent form

against Brian Lochore's All Blacks in the summer of 1970; his domination of the line-out continued and he was glad to reverse that 1965 defeat. Then, after many years of being adversaries, the South African was pleased to be paired with Colin Meads in the second row during the RFU's centenary celebrations in 1971; it was a fitting tribute to two of the finest forwards of all time. The Springbok made his final five international appearances in the wins over France and Australia in 1972. The lock had only suffered eight defeats in thirty-eight games, a South African record jointly held with Jan Ellis.

Frik du Preez had proved himself a forward in the finest Springbok traditions; his fortés were his line-out jumping and his powerful running with the ball in his hands – his country has produced none finer.

Graham Price

One-third of the legendary 'Pontypool Front-row' Graham Price was the most talented prop on the world scene in the late seventies. An introverted Welshman not noted for his long conversations, his work on the field was always accomplished with the minimum of fuss and the maximum effect. From his international debut in early 1975 until the end of the decade, Price did not miss a major match for either Wales or the British Lions. A former schoolboy international, he matured quickly in the toughest company, where experience and technique are the name of the game. And as his skills at tight-head were consolidated, Price's enterprising play in the loose became an essential part of Wales's ball-winning tactics.

As a no-nonsense prop, Price has troubled the world's best and he very quickly established world-wide respect with his expert technique and strength. Normally, promotion to an international front-

row is a gradual and slow process; the secrets of this 'union' are guarded jealously and are not given away lightly to the young. But Price's exceptional talent can be judged from the fact that he was just twenty-three when selected for Wales and only twenty-five when he returned home from battling with the All Blacks, conclusively confirmed as the world's number one tight-head prop. He now has the capacity to consolidate his position well into the eighties.

Although he is the most talented of the 'Pontypool Front-row', it is as a trio that the three—Price, Bobby Windsor and Charlie Faulkner—have achieved world fame. After the end of the 1979 International Championship, they had harnessed their talents as a unit 19 times for their country. And for 12 of those matches, their club captain, Terry Cobner, was with them in the Welsh pack. Their intimate knowledge of each other's game, especially as all four had come under the special influence of Pontypool's coach Ray Prosser, was a great benefit to Wales and, in 1977, to the British Lions. Bobby 'Duke' Windsor and Charlie Faulkner are two of Rugby's favourite characters and the 'Pontypool Front-row' will live on, long after even Graham Price has retired.

Graham Price's personal success has also been a time of tremendous achievements by Wales. In his first twenty international championship matches, he had to suffer the grave disappointment of defeat only three times; and to compensate, in his first five seasons, Wales won four championships, four Triple Crowns and two Grand Slams. (The magnitude of that honours' list is emphasised when you know that Scotland last won the Triple Crown in 1938, Ireland in 1949 and England in 1960; Wales won it four consecutive years, beginning in 1976.)

Not a bad record for a soldier's son, born in Egypt in 1951, although he returned to Britain shortly after his birth. His Rugby ability first showed itself at the West Monmouth grammar school from where he also played for the Welsh Secondary Schools in

Graham Price, playing for the Lions against Fiji in 1977, is the outstanding prop to appear on the world scene in the past decade.

1969 and 1970. Even before he left school, Price had appeared in Pontypool's first team and soon after, he was joined by Windsor and Faulkner, and one of Rugby's great institutions was born.

Price had to miss the Gwent match against Ian Kirkpatrick's All Blacks because of injury, but later appeared for Wales B and was then selected to make his international debut in January, 1975. France, as the opposition in the cauldron of Parc des Princes, is not the easiest of starts, but Price

had five of those who had appeared with him for Wales B a month earlier also making their debuts that day – they were Ray Gravell, Steve Fenwick, John Bevan, Trevor Evans, and, of course, Charlie Faulkner. It was the Pontypool Front-row's first Test performance, and with

135

Cobner in the pack, the club had four representatives in the forwards.

Nobody could have wished for a better start. In Mervyn Davies' first game as captain, his side won 25-10 and Price capped it all by running seventy yards in support of a kick ahead and was rewarded with an injury-time try to celebrate his first cap. Although they were defeated by Scotland, it was a championship year for Wales when they crushed Ireland 32-4 in the final match. The Pontypool connection were pleased when Charlie Faulkner scored one of the tries, because all of the famous four had now scored in two seasons of international Rugby. Pontypool's triumph was completed when they also carried off the Welsh club championship that year.

The quartet were at the heart of their country's Grand Slam success the following year, although Price had to leave the field with a scratched eye in the final game, against France. The 'Pontypool Front-row' was further disrupted the next season. Being out of favour with the selectors followed by injury meant Faulkner was missing; this led to him not being selected with his three team-mates for the Lions' trip to New Zealand in the summer of 1977. But Faulkner's replacement in the Welsh team, Clive Williams, was later injured himself and the Pontypool prop flew out to re-form one of Rugby's most famous combinations. Price's reputation as the world's best was cemented as he drilled prop after prop into the New Zealand mud; even the All Black Test props were made to look like novices. Although the series was lost, the Lions' pack gained domination and the front-row of Price, Peter Wheeler and Fran Cotton saw off New Zealand's finest.

The 'Pontypool Front-row' were back in occupation for another Grand Slam year the

Graham Price showing the full effects of the British Lions' battle against the All Blacks in the second Test at Christchurch in 1977.

136

following season, before touring Australia with the national side. It was a transitional tour for Wales – there was no Gareth Edwards or Phil Bennett. Yet, despite losing both internationals, it produced young players like Terry Holmes and Gareth Davies who would lead Wales into the next decade. It was a rough tour and Price had to leave the field in the second Test with a broken jaw, but he recovered quickly to play his full part in the next international season. It was another Triple Crown year and with twenty-four caps the Pontypool prop was able to look back on a very successful five years at the top. Now, Graham Price can look forward to dominating the world scene for a few years more.

John Pullin

England's most capped player, John Pullin led his country to a memorable hat-trick of victories in 1972 and 1973. The seventies was a poor decade for England in terms of results, but those three triumphs are more than any other country in the northern hemisphere has ever managed. The wins were over the three Rugby giants from the other side of the equator – South Africa, New Zealand and Australia – and the achievement was all the more significant because the first two were beaten on their own soil. Pullin was the England leader during this period and his quiet, dedicated handling of the players helped achieve the seemingly impossible.

The England tour to South Africa in 1972 came after they had been whitewashed – losing all four games – in the International Championship for the first time, and in the run-up to the 1973 Test against the All Blacks, all three provincial matches were lost. Despite this, they became the first home country to win in either Springbok or All Black strongholds, let alone both.

By this stage of his career, John Vivian Pullin was already a well-established and respected hooker on the world scene, having toured with the British Lions in 1968 and 1971, being an important member of the Test team on both occasions. Modest and unassuming, Pullin's style of play reflected his character – thorough, dedicated and accomplished with the minimum of fuss and show. He was the world's best hooker at his peak and was, perhaps prematurely, left out of the Lions' and England's thinking and discarded when he still had much to offer both.

No slouch in the loose, Pullin played a major role in the try scored by Gareth Edwards at the beginning of the 1973 Barbarians-All Blacks' thriller. After triple side-stepping, Phil Bennett fed JPR Williams, and it was Pullin who received the full-back's pass. The England hooker admits that if he had been playing for his country, he would have kicked the ball out of play. But skipper John Dawes told him to keep running and maintain the movement's momentum. This he did and the result was one of the most thrilling tries ever scored; all the more significant for the presence of the television cameras to record the event.

John Pullin was never taught the rudiments or art of hooking; he just picked up his technique as he went along. In his early days he had propped and this added to the experience which is invaluable and necessary to become a member of the front-row union. Unlike some other hookers at the time, Pullin was always a far-footed striker, considering the quality of the strike as important as the speed. Another of his considerable assets was that he was always superbly fit . . . training hard as well as working on the farm to keep himself in peak physical condition. And Pullin's skill as a captain was as effective as his hooking; he had the rare ability of being able to motivate and inspire even the veterans in the side who had seen it all before and he could encourage the newcomers to feel a part of the team and to play to their potential.

John Pullin at the front of a line-out in the game against France in 1973, a year when he led England to victory over the All Blacks in New Zealand.

All his school, club and county Rugby were played in the West Country, an area of England which will always be associated with his name. He was a member of the Bristol side that reached the final of the 1973 RFU Club Knock-out final, but the England hooker badly tore his knee ligaments in the opening minutes and Bristol never recovered – replacements were not allowed at that time. Pullin was at the centre of the Gloucestershire pack that appeared in eight County Championship finals, beginning in 1970, winning four of them, in the next nine years. After going to Thornbury grammar school, Pullin studied at the Royal Agricultural College at Cirencester. While

there, he joined the Bristol club at the age of eighteen in 1959. It was a playing association that was to last twenty years.

Pullin was learning his trade as he went along and, having served his apprenticeship, his potential was beginning to show and he won his first England cap in 1966, against Wales at Twickenham. Pullin was one of six new players in that side, another being Harlequin Jeremy Spencer in his one and only game for England. It was not a happy day for scrum-half or hooker and the home pack suffered many problems as Wales won. It was the hooker's last international for a couple of years. Although he appeared in the trials the next year and toured Canada with the national side that summer, Pullin had to wait until 1968 for his recall.

This time, with Bristol colleague Bill Redwood at scrum-half, he found his rhythm and a permanent place in England's

front-row. He consolidated his new status by appearing in three Tests on the 1968 Lions' tour of South Africa, a country he visited the following year with the Barbarians. The South African connection continued when Pullin scored a try in England's 11-8 win over the Springboks at Twickenham in 1969. The only country he wanted to prove himself against now was New Zealand and he received his chance when he was selected for John Dawes' Lions in 1971. Pullin played in all four Tests on that tour, confirming his position as the world's best. A week before the opening international, Pullin was expecting to be sandwiched between Sandy Carmichael and Ray McLoughlin for the Test series. But, after the 'battle' at Canterbury, although he still found himself between a Scotsman and Irishman, it was Ian McLauchlan and Sean Lynch as the first choices had to return

England's captain John Pullin feeds back to scrum-half Jan Webster in the 1974 game between England and France, a special non-international organised to raise money for the relatives of those who died in the Paris air disaster that year returning from the England–France game.

home injured. Pullin adjusted immediately to his new props and the new-look front-row caused the All Blacks many problems in the Tests. John Pullin had the invaluable knack of fitting between props of any size and fulfilling his hooking requirements perfectly.

By 1972 Pullin was an automatic choice for any side he was qualified to play for and his dedicated attitude made him an ideal choice to lead his country. The first leg of England's memorable hat-trick was achieved at Ellis Park in Johannesburg in 1972, when Alan Morley's try and Sam Doble's conversion and four penalty goals had brought a totally unexpected victory. Yet, it was no more remarkable than the one that England managed in New Zealand the following year. A proposed tour to Argentina was shelved and a four-game tour to New Zealand arranged in its place. With little preparation, England made the trip, lost their three provincial games and looked 'no-hopers' for the international. But Pullin rallied his men and they responded with one of the finest and most historic victories, 16-12, by an England side.

The hat-trick was completed when the Wallabies were defeated at Twickenham in November of the same year, 20-3. So, in less than eighteen months, England had beaten all three major Rugby powers from the southern hemisphere, with John Pullin as their captain. This feat is all the more remarkable because of their disastrous results at the time in the Championship.

John Pullin will have special cause to remember the 1974 game against Wales at Twickenham. When he led England out, it marked his thirty-fifth cap for his country, beating 'Budge' Rogers' record, and made the Bristol hooker England's most-capped player of all time. But, although that day also saw a rare defeat for the Welsh, it was probably the match that cost Pullin a place on the 1974 Lions' tour to South Africa. The England front-row did not have a happy day and Pullin lost his hooking duel with the Welsh newcomer Bobby Windsor.

After seeming a certainty all season for the Lions' team, Pullin was missing when the thirty names were announced for the visit. He was a surprise omission and that bad performance in the final game before selection gave him no chance to prove his case to the selectors. And the following season saw another 'young pretender'—this time it was Peter Wheeler who was at Pullin's heels, literally, for the England number two spot. It was a tussle the newcomer won in 1976, although Pullin was still of top international class as he proved with England in Australia in 1975.

The Bristol hooker finished his career for England at the Parc des Princes in March, 1976; it was his forty-second cap, an England record he still holds. He had helped his country through some rough times and to some memorable victories. England, like Wales, have been more than fortunate in the quality of their hookers and they have had none finer than John Pullin.

Jean-Pierre Rives

Jean-Pierre Rives was the outstanding flanker in world Rugby in the second half of the seventies. Instantly recognisable by flowing blond hair, he seemed almost systematically to cover every inch of the field during a game. Lightning-quick with an exceptional positional sense, Rives is a whole-hearted performer whose level of consistency at international level is staggering. Even without his blond hair, he would be easily spotted as he is seldom far from the ball. After the split up of the famous French back row towards the end of the decade – Skrela through retirement and Bastiat because of injury – Rives was still as effective, hounding player and ball alike, ready to drive in to provide possession for France. His tackling can best be described as totally all-engulfing and he could never be accused of not taking the battle to the enemy.

Bastiat's injury also gave Rives the chance to lead his country and the flanker tried to re-introduce France's free-flowing style of running Rugby which they had abandoned towards the end of the seventies. Success could not be guaranteed immediately, but if Rives is allowed to remain in charge, then his influence will continue to be felt. He has always hated negative, ten-man Rugby, which spoils his and thousands of spectators' enjoyment. And Rives with the ball in his hands is a joy to watch, often worth a special study. He never relaxes and studying his play provides a rare insight into a very talented Rugby brain, as he assesses situations intuitively and reacts almost automatically and almost always correctly. But Rives is no robot; he follows the high tradition of creative French forwards.

After representing France at schoolboy, junior, university, Under-23 and B level, he burst upon the full scene in 1975 at the age of twenty-two. His high standard belied his inexperience in international Rugby, with a marvellous maurauding performance in only his second game, against Scotland. Within a season, Rives was recognised among the top flankers in world Rugby, with people perhaps wondering if he would burn himself out if he carried on as he had started.

In fact, the French flanker, who stood at five foot eleven and weighed just under thirteen stone, sustained those early impressions and more than fulfilled his promise. Not only his play, but his good looks and blond hair, attracted much attention, not least from young girl supporters whose fan letters helped swell his mail bag. This adulation did not appeal to Rives at all; neither did his nicknames 'The Golden Boy' or even 'The Blond Angel'.

French captain and flanker Jean-Pierre Rives in typical action during the England-France international at Twickenham in 1979.

The last half of the seventies was a very successful period for the French team in terms of results, although many decried their lack of their traditional style in winning. In Rives' first twenty-three internationals—until the end of 1979—France won seventeen of those games and only suffered defeats against Wales (twice) and England, Ireland and New Zealand. Rives had been on the winning side in five consecutive matches against Scotland.

The back-row combination with Rives, Jean-Pierre Bastiat and Jean-Claude Skrela became one of the best-known in Rugby circles and they worked very effectively together. Rives' relationship with Skrela

Jean-Pierre Rives on the attack against Wales in Cardiff in 1978; by the end of the seventies the French flanker, now captain, was getting his side to return to their former running, open style.

back-row played together for the last time in the final hurdle in their attempt to regain the Grand Slam, against Wales in Cardiff. But it was not to be; France's goal-kicking let them down, Wales won 16-7 and Skrela retired from international Rugby.

With Bastiat also missing through injury, Rives was left to carry on alone the following year and was given the captaincy of France. There were some teething problems that season as they tried to revert to their running style, but if he is allowed to carry on in charge, he will take French Rugby into the eighties playing traditional, unorthodox, imaginative Rugby. His success in the 1-1 series with New Zealand in 1979 helped his cause. It could be a fruitful period for France and spectators everywhere.

Ken Scotland

The adventurous running of Scottish full-back Ken Scotland from the last line of defence was more characteristic of the seventies than the late fifties when he began his international career. Scotland was a beautiful runner, but only survived at international level without being castigated by critics and opponents because of his complete mastery of the full-back's defensive arts. He was the all-round footballer, as suited to fly-half as he was to full-back, though he preferred not to play in the more crowded centre.

Possessing a footballing brain of rare insight, he read game situations instinctively and was able to assess the danger or calculated risk of counter-attacking out of defence. If he did find himself isolated, which was not very frequent, his superb punting of the ball with either foot would get him out of trouble. Scotland was

was almost telephatic, helped, no doubt, by the fact that they played their club Rugby together for Toulouse. The trio were at the centre of France's Grand Slam in 1977, but injury meant that Rives was missing when Graham Mourie's All Blacks visited France later that year. He recovered for the next championship campaign and the legendary

courageous in defence, his intelligence preventing him from ever being foolhardy, and
he had an exceptional temperament for the
big occasion; he knew instinctively what to
do and, perhaps more importantly, what
not to do. Being a beautifully-balanced
runner, he was able to beat opponents with
subtle changes of direction and pace. His
versatility was such that he played in every
back position, with the exception of wing, on
the 1959 Lions' tour of Australasia.

On that tour, although he preferred to use
a straight-on, toe-kicking action for shots at
goal, he would use the round-the-corner
style for longer attempts. Scotland is
accredited with, or in some of the more
traditional New Zealand circles accused of,
introducing that method to New Zealand.
Magnificently co-ordinated, he was a good
enough sportsman to have played cricket
for his country, although he always likes to
put the record straight by recounting: 'One
innings, three balls, no runs.'

Like seven other Scottish full-backs
before and since, Kenneth James Forbes

Scotland was educated at George Heriot's
School in Edinburgh. His Rugby prowess
had gained him representative honours for
Edinburgh Schools for three seasons and in
1954, he played for the Scottish Schoolboys
in the annual fixture against the English
Schoolboys at Richmond. After leaving
school, he spent his two year's national
service in the Army and soon made his mark
in service Rugby and was already an international before going to Cambridge University in the autumn of 1957, having been
capped during the 1957 International
Championship at the age of twenty. Those
four internationals that year, plus the two
trials, were the only games he played at full-
back that season, which only went to emphasise his tremendous versatility. He made his
debut in the unfriendly atmosphere of the
Colombes stadium in Paris, but emerged
unscathed and the hero of the day as he
kicked a penalty and a drop goal in
Scotland's 6-0 triumph.

With that appearance, Ken Scotland became only the second player in the history of

Rugby to have the honour of playing for the country of his name. John Ireland was the first when he played against England in 1876, but, unlike Ireland, Scotland made a winning debut and a memorable start to a distinguished career that was to see him established as his country's first-choice full-back for the next eight seasons.

Surprisingly, however, the new international suffered a dramatic loss of form at Cambridge and could not even command a place in the 'Varsity side. With this loss of form went his Scotland place and he only played once in 1958; he had come into the side for the Calcutta Cup after Robin Chisholm had been injured in the Irish match. That Calcutta Cup game against England was drawn and although he played seven times against the 'auld enemy', he was never to appear on the winning side, a fate shared by many of his colleagues at the time. (After defeating England 13-11 in 1950, Scotland had to wait until 1964 before recording their next win over the English). Once Scotland had put the disappointment of that 1957-58 season behind, his form and fortunes took a turn for the better and he was soon playing some of his best Rugby for Cambridge University, Scotland and, later in the summer of 1959, for the British Lions.

That Lions' tour established Scotland's reputation as one of the most noted attacking full-backs Rugby has ever seen. He played in five of the six Tests, missing the second game against New Zealand because of injury. Although he played in most of the back positions, it was as a full-back that the New Zealand crowds enjoyed him most.

He gave them plenty of warning of his ability, because in his first game in New Zealand against Hawkes Bay he ran in three successive tries from the full-back position. In all, he scored ten tries on the tour, which will always be remembered for the quality of

the British back play. Scotland was a vital link in the smooth running of their three-quarters; he made his excursions from defence either with the ball in his hands after fielding a badly-aimed kick ahead or coming into the line to provide the overlap and space for wings like Peter Jackson, Tony O'Reilly and John Young, giving them opportunities they did not need asking twice to take. After appearing in the first two Tests at full-back, Scotland was in the centre when the Lions won the final game, 9-6, a victory for their enterprising back-play.

Although the early sixties were not a particularly successful time for Scottish international Rugby, their eponymous full-back would guarantee to impress whether his side was winning or not. And Scotland is a name that will always be associated with the famous London Scottish sevens of the sixties when they won five out of six titles at the Middlesex Sevens tournament. Scotland's skills blended perfectly with a talented, footballing side that set new standards in the art of playing sevens.

Yet he played only in the opening two wins in that golden era for London Scottish; work commitments took him to Leicester and he served the club there with great distinction, becoming a great favourite with the 'Tigers' supporters. After the 1963 International Championship, Ken Scotland only made one more appearance for his country, against France in Paris in 1965, to give him a total of twenty-seven caps. That French game brought him level with another Heriot's member, Dan Drysdale, as Scotland's most-capped full-back. Both had played in that position twenty-five times; two of Ken Scotland's caps had been at fly-half and one of Drysdale's twenty-six was against the 1927 New South Wales side, 'The Waratahs'.

Scotland was one of the finest footballers ever produced by Scotland or any other country. His class and control were obvious to all those who saw him; in many ways, this full-back was ahead of his time with regard to the general attitude towards the defensive duties of the last line of defence and before the law changes which brought greater freedom and the atmosphere of attacking Rugby; but Scotland was a player of any era; his many talents were too good to ever be bogged down or restricted by any outside influences.

Bob Scott

Bob Scott was the most accomplished footballer to play full-back for the All Blacks in the past fifty years. Although never as dramatic a match-winner as Don Clarke proved to be, he nevertheless brought a rare style and poise to the last line of defence. Always showing remarkable balance, he would thrill crowds by his ability to get out of the tightest corners; a jink here, a side-step there, a shuffle of the feet and he was free. But of all his qualities, it was his positional sense that was the finest. He was very rarely found wanting when fielding kicks ahead, and then would either return the kick with interest or launch a counter-attack. In addition, his kicking, whether out of hand or at goal, was of international standard although he never dominated Test series in the way that Don Clarke was to do in the late fifties and the early sixties.

'Cool, calm and collected' is the best way of describing Scott's style at full-back . . . no matter the pressure or the difficult conditions, Scott was adept at coping with all problems and was the rock of the New Zealand defence for the decade after the end of the war.

The player did not have the happiest of childhoods. Born in Wellington just after the First World War, Robert William Henry Scott spent some of his early days at the Salvation Army home in Masterton. His father had been badly wounded in the Gallipoli landing and was a chronic invalid. Scott himself contracted polio and there was a long recovery period. Still, he was fit enough to play amateur Rugby League for Ponsonby at the age of 14, but returned to the Union code while a serviceman in the Army during the Second World War. He was able to do this because of a special dispensation allowed to the forces, a dispensation that was to prove very beneficial for All Black Rugby over the years as Scott, time and time again, proved his worth.

His first major tour with the Kiwis, who proved so popular in Britain immediately after the war, did not see him dominate the full-back berth as he was to do later. The other full-back on that visit was Herb Cooke, a fine player who was later to find fame with the Leeds Rugby League team. While Scott was immaculate in his play at the back, Cooke was just as likely to be caught way out of position; but when he found the ball in his hands, Cooke was the most flamboyant of performers, creating havoc in the opposition defences with his exciting running and thrilling the crowds wherever he went. Both were also excellent kickers, but it was obvious to all that Scott was still learning his trade and it was only a matter of time before he left Cook trailing in his wake. Already prematurely balding, it was his class on the field that caught the British Rugby public's eye as much as his lack of hair; the side, on the whole, had a very successful tour, beating Wales at Cardiff.

Scott was selected for New Zealand's first international after the war, against Australia, and kicked five conversions out of seven in the All Blacks' 31-8 win. And by the time he was a member of the national touring party that visited South Africa in 1949, Scott was already established as one of the top full-backs in world Rugby. In fact, he was being compared to the legendary George Nepia, who played in every match when the 'Invincibles' visited Britain in 1924. That was praise indeed and a measure of the high esteem in which he was held.

Still, in many ways, that South African

tour was a disappointment for Scott and for New Zealand. For only the second time, they lost all four Tests. Scott's general play was magnificent, but he had a terrible time and terrible luck with his place kicking. It wasn't that he was a bad goal-kicker or was kicking badly, but every time a match hung in that precarious stage when three points would turn the game, Scott's kicks would just drift past the post or even bounce back into play, anything, in fact, rather than fly over the bar. Although he more than compensated with his field play and left with the critics hailing him as the finest full-back to visit South Africa, he was annoyed and disappointed that his goal-kicking form, which would have been the icing on the cake, eluded him.

Scott maintained his form and excelled against the British Lions' side that visited New Zealand the following year. They considered him in much the same way that the Springboks did. His catching, kicking, tackling and positional play surpassed even the high standards he had set himself in South Africa, and Scott was at the heart of the New Zealand victory in the Test series. Scott was at the top; he was a great favourite with the New Zealand crowds and won respect in Australia, South Africa and Britain. So after travelling the world, he announced his retirement from international Rugby after that series against the British Lions. Scott was leaving Rugby as number one and he was leaving New Zealand with the problem of replacing a world-class full-back. Yet, when the fourth All Blacks under the leadership of Bob Stuart visited Britain in 1953-54, Bob Scott was there at full-back. The New Zealand selectors had prevailed on him to return to international football. That he did, and the All Blacks and the British Rugby supporters were very grateful. Even at the age of 33, he was the model of impeccable full-back play.

He played in all the internationals, his appearance against France being his seventeenth and final match for New Zealand.

Bob Scott breaks out of defence for Auckland in their match against the 1950 British Lions, which the visitors won 32-9.

Having come out of retirement to play on this tour, his quick return to top form emphasised his class. Now, he was even more dangerous in attack; and by the end of the tour, the home sides were taking special measures to isolate the New Zealand full-back from his All Black colleagues. But there was no denying his calming and mature influence on the rest of the party and he was one of the outstanding personalities on that tour.

His final game in Britain was the traditional match against the Barbarians. After Scott had made an uncustomary error and allowed a Baa-Baa try, he immediately made amends by dropping a fifty-yard goal and then treated the Cardiff crowd to what many consider to be one of the finest individual displays ever seen on a Rugby field. The Cardiff crowd are never slow to recognise greatness and this almost bald thirty-three year old was carried shoulder high from the pitch.

Scott announced his retirement for the

second time, and this time it was for good. As in 1950, he was going out at the top of his trade; he set standards that every New Zealander has tried to follow since; none has quite come up to them. Not that full-backs the class of Bob Scott appear every year or even every generation. You would not expect them to; his gifts were rare and he used them intelligently; it is fortunate that he shared them with Rugby supporters everywhere.

Richard Sharp

Captain of England's last championship side (up to 1979) Richard Sharp was a fly-half whose poise and grace have not been seen in that position for England since he left the international scene in 1963. He did make a belated curtain-call in 1967 for the game against Australia, but that game, perhaps fortunately, is rarely taken into account when assessing his talents. He won thirteen caps from his debut in 1960 until the 1963 International Championship; with the one cap against the Wallabies four years later.

That final game in 1963 – against Scotland – contained what many regard as Sharp's finest moment on the international field and ensured that the Scots would always remember his name with rather less than real affection. Although England went into the game with two wins and a draw – against Ireland – in the championship and were consoled that they had not been beaten at Twickenham by the Scots since 1938, many had the feeling that the invaders could triumph that day. There was a 70,000 crowd, including the then Prime Minister, Harold Macmillan, to watch Scotland set about the task of their first post-war win at HQ; and things seemed to be going their way as the visitors swept into an 8-0 lead with little response from England. Eventually the home side replied through a Drake-Lee try, which Wilcox converted, and they turned round only three points adrift.

All was left to play for, but within five minutes of the second half, the tall, blond fly-half had turned the tables. Sharp had not had a particularly impressive first-half, but with one run he became the hero of the day and will always be remembered when the 1963 Calcutta Cup is mentioned. England won a set scrum forty yards out, Simon Clarke fed Sharp who ran outside the Scottish flanker, Ross. Having escaped his attentions, Sharp sold perfect dummy scissors to centres Phillips and Weston and ran between them heading for the opposition line.

There was only full-back Blaikie to beat and, with England wing Jim Roberts outside him, it seemed a simple case of drawing the defender before passing to his wing. But as he neared the full-back he could see Blaikie was in two minds, so he threw a huge dummy which Blaikie 'bought' completely, and Sharp was over for one of the most famous tries ever scored at Twickenham. Wilcox converted to give England the Calcutta Cup and the championship. Sharp recalls his moment of decision very clearly. 'I had no choice for my mind was made up for me. Blaikie made the mistake of not going for the man in possession. I was almost on top of him when I realised that, although he was physically in front of me, his mind was on Jim Roberts. The memory of that moment is still vivid. I knew I did the right thing.'

That one moment of Sharp magic had changed the course of the game. In what many thought was his last international, it was a timely reminder of the talents of one of the most skilful, attacking fly-halves in the game's history.

Richard Adrian William Sharp was born in Mysore, Southern India, in 1938 and was the son of a mining engineer who had played Rugby for Wasps, the club that Richard and his brother Nigel joined at birth. But the family's roots were in Cornwall and it was there that the future England fly-half had his schooling. His first club Rugby was played with Redruth, one of two clubs that are always associated with Richard Sharp. The other is, of course, the Wasps, and Sharp's introduction to the London club was a rather bizarre affair. With his father and brother, he watched Camborne entertain the Wasps on Good Friday on the London club's West Country tour in 1957. The Wasps were short of players and here were two young and willing recruits, albeit only for the Easter holiday.

And so it came to pass that the brothers played for Redruth against Lloyds Bank on the Saturday afternoon, left the field and travelled in their father's car, still in their kit, to Penzance, where they turned out for the Wasps against the local club in the evening. Both games were won. Yet, to show a complete division of loyalties, the Sharp brothers turned out *for* Redruth *against* Wasps on Easter Monday!

In the autumn of 1959 Richard Sharp travelled up to Oxford to study at Balliol College where he set his sights on a Blue. He missed much of the first term's matches through injury and proved his fitness only in the game against London Scottish–the final game before the 'Varsity match–but this was enough to ensure his selection for the Oxford side by skipper Malcom Phillips. It was the first of three Blues for Sharp, but the only time he was on the winning side.

Already the newcomer was challenging for the England spot, but such was the form of Bev Risman, a talented Lion, that the undergraduate could do little but bide his time. Sharp was wondering on the Thursday before the opening England international against Wales whether to travel to Twickenham and watch the game. His mind was made up for him when he returned to his digs that night to find a telegram from the England selectors asking him to report for training at Rosslyn Park the next day. Once there, he learnt that Risman had pulled a leg muscle and that he was to make his England debut the next day. First Sharp

England fly-half Richard Sharp tussles with Welsh flanker Brian Cresswell during the former's dream debut in the 1960 international.

149

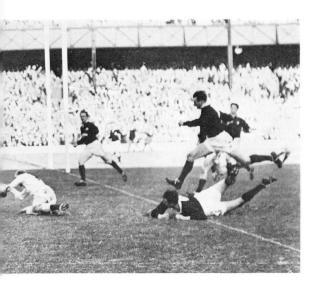

Richard Sharp dives over for his most famous try, the match-winning effort against the Scots in the 1963 Calcutta Cup match.

made contact with his scrum-half – Dickie Jeeps – and the pair had their first practice together at the team run-out. So, despite being the home side, England were only slight favourites – they were fielding new half-backs who had never played together and, in addition, the national side had not scored a try for twenty-three months.

But that Saturday in 1960 provided a dream debut for Richard Sharp; he was completely at ease and was soon showing the Twickenham crowd his gliding, running skills as he sped past Hadyn Morgan and tore holes in the Welsh defence. He made the second England try when he performed a dummy-scissors with Phillips to send Roberts over for the try. If the characters seem familiar, the trio were to play the major roles in that classic 1963 Calcutta Cup try. Roberts' try was his second of the game as England rushed into a 14-0 lead at the interval, eventually winning 14-6.

It was a great start for England in the championship and the perfect beginning to Sharp's international career. It was to prove a memorable year for him as he was again in scintillating form in the 21-12 win over Scotland at Murrayfield. As Ireland had already been beaten, the Triple Crown belonged to England for the thirteenth and, up to 1979, the last time. That year, England shared the points (3-3) and the championship with France. Although Sharp continued to show occasional flashes, including an excellent kicking display for the Barbarians against the 1961 Springboks, he gained the reputation of not being consistent and his play was a bit 'hot and cold'.

Perhaps too much was expected of him; perhaps the opposition were able to control him after his initial surprise had passed. That is only partly the truth – his perception was still good enough to rip open an international defence for one last time in 1963.

Injuries were much more at the heart of the problem. Despite missing the 1962 game against Scotland through influenza, the Lions' selectors knew he was going to be a valuable member of their squad for the summer tour to South Africa. As for Sharp, he saw it as a perfect setting for his skills. 'Certainly I have never played better or enjoyed my Rugby more than in the first few weeks of touring South Africa. Everything was going well for us; we were in superb physical shape; the grounds were firm and dry; there were good players all around – and we were winning matches. If one can't play at one's best in such conditions, I don't think one ever will.'

Unfortunately, his tour, to all intents and purposes, was finished in the sixth game, against Northern Transvaal. Most of those who witnessed the tackle by Mannie Roux after five minutes were in little doubt that it was late. Sharp was hospitalised with a fractured jaw and did not return to the tour for six weeks, by which time the series had been decided in the home side's favour. His absence had been a major factor contributing to those defeats.

When he returned home, Sharp took over the England captaincy from Dickie Jeeps, who had announced his retirement. An almost brand-new England pack had spurred the visitors to victory in Cardiff and then Sharp's moment of inspiration against the Scots clinched the Championship. It is doubtful whether Sharp or anyone else at Twickenham that day would have guessed that England would enter the eighties without adding another title to their total.

Sharp retired after that season, being unable to tour New Zealand with the national team in that summer of 1963. But the selectors saw fit to bring him back as fly-half and captain against Australia in 1967. It was not a successful day for Sharp or England as they went down 11-23 to the Wallabies, whose half-backs, Catchpole and Hawthorne, were in commanding form that day. It has always been an unfortunate tendency for selectors to call up former heroes when in trouble; it does little service to the players, who, more than most, deserve to be left in peace.

Fortunately, that Australian game is almost forgotten and most regard Sharp's performance as the 'Hammer of the Scots' in 1963 as the real finale to his distinguished career. A mark of his status in the game is that, at his best, he stood way above those around him, even on the international field; he was one of the masters of the dummy and the outside swerve; he could make the toughest, hungriest flanker look naive and walk through a hard-tackling centre combination. Perhaps he lacked real consistency at international level, but his moments of brilliance are what linger in the memory of Rugby fans everywhere.

Piet du Toit

The controversial South African prop of the late fifties and early sixties Piet du Toit was one of the strongest scrummagers to play the game, but his technique led to claims of illegal tactics. His strength was legendary and he had the ability to disrupt opposition front-rows, even at international level. He

would direct his push downwards and inwards, often causing the scrums to collapse. Of course, to shove inwards at an angle was contrary to the laws and du Toit was frequently in trouble with referees. Yet he was the cornerstone of the Springbok packs during his fourteen caps, which were all consecutive and began in the international against France in 1958.

Although his career was relatively short – working demands on his farm forcing an early retirement from the international arena – Pieter Stephanus du Toit impressed as a major figure in two international series. He played an important role in the 1960 Tests against the All Blacks in South Africa, when he caused the legendary New Zealand captain, Wilson Whineray, all sorts of problems; the Springboks eventually won the fourth Test and the series. Then he travelled to Britain and France with Avril Malan's 1960-61 side, who won four and drew the other international.

The South African pack was a feared unit and du Toit a vital member of the eight that bulldozed through opposition forwards. Du

Although his international career spanned only a relatively short time, Piet du Toit was one of the strongest scrummagers ever to play for South Africa.

Toit was very much the old-style prop, concentrating on his role in the set pieces. Not for him the modern trend to be seen running with the ball in his hand and supporting in loose play, as he could in no way be described as quick around the field. It was a very successful period for the Springboks; they were defeated only twice in du Toit's fourteen games, and both those losses came in his first four internationals.

Du Toit had matured early for a prop and quickly gained international recognition. He was a member of the 1956 Springbok party and, although he did not play in any of the Tests, it was an invaluable experience for a twenty-year-old youngster. Later that year, du Toit came to Britain with the Western Province Universities side. His South African debut was not the happy affair he had hoped it would be and in the two-Test series with France, the first was drawn and the second lost. The French had responded well to the challenge, but the Springboks

have always had a great deal of trouble with France's unpredictable style of running Rugby. It was all the more effective in 1958, because the French forwards were well organised by Lucien Mias.

The new prop had to wait another two years before his first victory in the green jersey with the gold Springbok badge. Du Toit had already caused All Black captain Whineray many problems in the Boland provincial game, with the New Zealand skipper very critical of du Toit's methods. All through the series, referees had trouble keeping the front-rows settled with the All Blacks trying to hold ground and keep on their feet as du Toit was disrupting their push and formation. The fruit farmer was penalised by the South African referee not only for collapsing scrums, but for also not

Piet du Toit, seen here playing against France in 1961, was one of the oustanding successes on that Springbok tour.

allowing the ball to come into the tunnel properly. The Springboks won an exciting Test series and du Toit's reputation as the hard man of South African Rugby was established. Even allowing for the validity of the complaints of his methods, there was no doubting the immense power in the neck, shoulders and back of this prop, and he is still widely recognised as one of the strongest men ever to play international Rugby.

Discussion of the way he had ground down the best of New Zealand's props preceded him on his tour to Britain, so British opposition was not exactly looking forward to the confrontation. Du Toit went through the tour without much trouble from his opponents or British referees who seemed satisfied with his technique. He was penalised towards the end of the visit and his play came under closer scrutiny from that time. That South African pack was one of the best to have visited Britain, gaining the upper hand over most forwards they encountered. The internationals also went South Africa's way, with a 0-0 draw against France stopping them achieving complete success in the Tests.

Du Toit was to play in three more internationals, all in 1961, once against Ireland and twice versus Australia, but he was missing when Arthur Smith's Lions visited in 1962. He had decided to call it a day and concentrate on his fruit farming. Du Toit was a difficult man to replace, having proved himself one of his country's strongest and most forceful props. For sheer strength, he had few equals.

Kel Tremain

The New Zealand flanker Kel Tremain was one of the best loose forwards ever seen on a Rugby field. He was an All Black for almost a decade, setting a high standard of play he maintained throughout. Tremain's particular forte was in broken play, and he was exceptionally dangerous near the opponent's line, earning a reputation as one of the game's top try-scoring forwards. He scored nine tries for New Zealand in his thirty-eight appearances for his country, a tally for a forward only bettered by the man who replaced Tremain in the New Zealand side, Ian Kirkpatrick. Kel Tremain twice scored in three consecutive games for the All Blacks, in 1961-62 and in the opening three Tests of the 1965 series against the South Africans.

The flanker epitomised all that is good and expected of New Zealand forwards – strong, hard, with good handling and the conviction that anything else other than total effort would be a disgrace to the black jersey with the silver fern, or, indeed, any other jersey he wore. He was not a force in the line-out, admitting to being a poor jumper, but in all other departments he was supreme. When a defence had been hard to crack, it was invariably Tremain who would find the gap with his aggressive and determined running with the ball.

Tremain is fondly remembered in Britain where he toured in 1963-64 and 1967, playing in all the British Tests on both Whineray's and Lochore's tours. Respected the world over, Tremain was a member of one of the finest and most powerful units of all time – the All Blacks' pack of the mid-sixties. It reigned supreme, providing the platform for one of the most successful periods in the history of New Zealand's Rugby, which has never been noted for providing poor fifteens.

Born in 1938 and educated at Auckland Grammar School, Kelvin Robert Tremain played for three different New Zealand provinces – Southland (1957), Manawatu (1958) and Canterbury (1959) – before he made his international debut for New Zealand. Before his career was over, he was also to play for Auckland and Hawkes Bay. The six-foot-one-and-a-half-inch, fifteen-and-a-half-stone Tremain first turned out in a New

Zealand trial and went on tour with the NZ Under-23 side to Japan in 1958.

The following year saw the visit of Ronnie Dawson's Lions and Kel Tremain's first cap. He was brought into the side to replace Pickering after the All Blacks' welcome, but unsatisfactory, 18-17 win in the first Test. The newcomer impressed with his energetic debut and it was generally recognised that here was someone special who would be on the New Zealand scene for many years to come. With the All Blacks clinching the series after three internationals and Tremain acknowledged as the outstanding forward, he was an automatic choice for the 1960 tour to South Africa. It was a hard series, with the forward battle dominating proceedings, giving Tremain less opportunity than he would have liked to excel in the loose, which was proving to be the strongest aspect of his game. Although the Tests were lost 2-1, it was a close run thing and Tremain returned home with his reputation enhanced and his position on the side of the New Zealand scrum confirmed.

After seven internationals Tremain, strangely, had still to open his try-scoring account. He put the matter right in the 1961 series against France. After missing the first international because of injury, he reappeared in the second game which was played in a howling gale. Tremain charged down Lacaze's clearance in the second half and scored ten yards in from the corner to level the scores; and Don Clarke's amazing conversion gave the All Blacks victory. Another try by Tremain followed in the next game as France were given a 32-3 drubbing. And it was three in three internationals for the flanker when he charged down another clearing kick to score in the opening Test against the 1962 Wallabies.

It was as a senior member of the party that he was selected to tour Britain and France under Wilson Whineray in 1963. Slightly sluggish at the beginning of the tour, Kel Tremain regained full fitness and formed a devastating back-row with Nathan

and Graham. There was no stopping the All Blacks' machine on this visit and only a 0-0 draw against Scotland deprived them of victories over all five countries from the International Championship. Tremain scored the winning try against Ireland and then turned in one of his finest performances, against England at Twickenham. The day belonged to him and the All Black flanker produced form that few would have been able to emulate.

It was a golden era for All Black Rugby and Tremain played in all the games in the 1965 Test victories over the Springboks and the 1966 crushing of the British Lions. That 1965 South African series brought him another hat-trick of tries in the first three games. He scored another in the second Test against Campbell-Lamerton's Lions and his final All Black try in the 1967 game against Australia at Wellington. It is interesting to

Kel Tremain, one of the All Blacks' best post-war flankers, feeds the ball out in an international against the Wallabies in 1962.

note that he played in seven try-less internationals before scoring for New Zealand and, after nine tries in the next twenty-four games, played out his final seven games for New Zealand, again without scoring.

His last major tour was with Lochore's 1967 party. Living legend that he was, Tremain found himself faced with the strong challenge for his position by Ian Kirkpatrick. 'Kirkie' had come out as understudy to Brian Lochore and had not been expected to play a major part on the visit. Again, after a slow start, Tremain recaptured his best form. Although he was replaced by Kirkpatrick for the French Test, he was back in the side for the game against Scotland. Kirkpatrick had performed well against France and scored a try, but a broken nose meant he could not be considered for the Murrayfield game. It was an unexpected chance Tremain did not have to be asked twice to take. With a superb display, he re-established his claims, possession being nine-tenths of the law. The newcomer was not going to take Tremain's

place that easily. Tremain played on the flank in the three-Test series versus France in 1968 and he retired as the second most-capped All Black behind Colin Meads.

He is still in third spot, his thirty-eight appearances being one less than his successor Ian Kirkpatrick notched up. Both, in fact, played thirty-six times as an All Black flanker, Tremain also playing twice at No. 8 and Kirkpatrick three times. Ian Kirkpatrick also overtook Tremain's record of nine tries by a New Zealand forward, ending up with sixteen.

Kel Tremain was an outstanding ambassador for his country; his behaviour was as immaculate on the field as it was friendly off it. Whenever that All Blacks' pack of the sixties is talked about and discussed, which is fairly frequently, Kel Tremain's name is prominent as an example of all that is good and skilful in New Zealand forward play.

Kel Tremain, doing what the All Blacks were best at in the mid-sixties, picking the ball up from a scrum and driving forward.

Dawie de Villiers, the South African scrum-half and captain, kicks ahead in the first Test against the 1968 British Lions.

Dawie de Villiers

A scrum-half, Dawie de Villiers took over the captaincy of South Africa at the age of twenty-four and after only three Test appearances. A very talented footballer, he proved the ideal diplomat to lead his country during the late sixties with all its political pressures. A maturity beyond his years plus a friendly, generous disposition enabled him to cope with situations and arguments not normally encountered by international Rugby captains. He was instantly identified by his blond hair and boyish good looks and these features were part of the world Rugby scene for almost a decade. His style was very much that of the running scrum-half with a devastating break and, of course, the hard grounds of South Africa brought out the best in his Rugby; in contrast, in the mud of

Britain and New Zealand his service was sometimes rather erratic and not so effective.

Dawie de Villiers would have won many more than twenty-five caps had he not been frequently troubled by injury; when he was absent, his side missed his tactical appreciation as well as his control at scrum-half. By the time he retired in 1970, he was his country's most experienced captain, leading South Africa in twenty-two games. De Villiers had carried a responsibility far in excess of a normal Rugby skipper; in addition, his position as a minister of religion gave him the confidence and patience to cope with opposition on and off the field.

He was often compared with his contemporaries at scrum-half in the late sixties — Ken Catchpole, Gareth Edwards, Roger Young, Chris Laidlaw, John Hipwell, Sid Going. Perhaps he was not quite the all-rounder that some of the others were and perhaps he set himself too high standards. In trying for extra length in his pass, he would spend that split-second too long in his wind-up and he would frequently have kicks charged down. But, on his day, he was equal to the best and his tactical appreciation and inspiration to teams were large bonuses.

David Jacobus de Villiers, born in 1940, was educated in Cape Town at the Belville High School. This five-foot-seven, eleven-and-a-half-stone scrum-half made his Springbok debut against the British Lions in 1962. It was a busy year for him; studying at Stellenbosch University for divinity he played for the Southern Universities, then also Western Province, Junior Springboks and finally the Springboks in the final two Tests against the Lions.

Although his promise was noted, he was missing from the international scene for two years and at one time it looked as if he might be restricted to only those two appearances. A serious knee injury brought the medical opinion: 'You'll never play again' – but he fought back and was selected as vice-captain for the short tour of Scotland and Ireland in 1964-65. Although he missed the Scottish Test in that disappointing tour, de Villiers was named captain of the 1965 Springbok party to visit New Zealand. His vice-captain was Nelie Smith, the other scrum-half. Both were fine players, which was just as well because injuries kept the captain out of three of the six internationals. A sprained ankle kept him out of the two Australian Tests, but he recovered for the first game against the All Blacks. The home side gained a controversial 6-3 win and it marked the Springboks' sixth defeat in a row. After missing the second Test, de Villiers returned to play perhaps his finest-ever game for his country in the third international.

There was still the general feeling that de Villiers' game was suited to the hard going only, but he proved the critics wrong on the treacherous surface of Lancaster Park, Christchurch. The series had seemed all over when the Springboks turned round 16-5 down; de Villiers took the reins and he inspired one of the finest recoveries ever

seen on a Rugby field; his players followed his example and the game was theirs 19-16. Wilson Whineray, New Zealand's captain, made the rare step of singling out a player for special praise, feeling that de Villiers' performance merited this mention. It was South Africa's only victory of the series, but the Springbok captain had made a great impact on the New Zealand public, who appreciated his friendly manner.

It was a disappointing period in terms of international results for South Africa, but they turned the corner in the 1967 series against France. Those four internationals plus the four the following summer against the British Lions brought five wins, two draws and only one defeat. De Villiers, now ordained as a clergyman in the Dutch Reform Church at Stellenbosch, stayed free of injury to inspire his side. South Africa's recovery was confirmed when they travelled to France in 1968-69, winning both Tests, before whitewashing Australia in 1969. But de Villiers severely injured a shoulder in the first game against the Wallabies and did not return until the fourth Test. Yet his influence was noticed and he was named South Africa's 'Sportsman of the Year'.

After that bad spell in the mid-sixties, South Africa's eleven games without defeat were very welcome and there were high hopes for the tour to Britain at the end of the decade. There were strong feelings inside Britain that this tour should not take place because of opposition to South Africa's apartheid system; captain de Villiers coped well with the problems, retaining a pleasant dignity at all times and remained the perfect diplomat at every occasion. While his own form was good, some of his party seemed to react to the outside pressures and found increasing difficulty in concentrating on their Rugby. On the playing side, the tour was somewhat of a disaster with defeats by Scotland and England and draws with Wales and Ireland; the captain was missing because of influenza from the match at Murrayfield.

Dawie de Villiers, who was the corner-stone of Springbok Rugby in the late sixties, breaks away in the 1968 series against the French.

While South Africa may have fallen from their previous high standing achieved on other British tours, the captain's position as a world-class scrum-half was confirmed. His final series in charge was against New Zealand, who visited South Africa in 1970, and the series brought the captain in contest with Chris Laidlaw and Sid Going. In a hard-fought series, the honours between the scrum-halves were about even, with de Villiers' team winning three of the four Tests. The scrum-half, after twenty-five internationals, announced his retirement, having led South Africa back to respectability in world terms. He returned to England in happier circumstances as a member of the world side that celebrated the RFU's centenary in 1971.

At the end of the seventies, he again returned to England, this time as his country's ambassador; he had changed little in appearance. Now, as then, he is proving a fine ambassador for his country and Rugby.

David Watkins

Fly-half David Watkins, after captaining Wales and the British Lions, went 'North' to become a Rugby League international. No country, in any position, has been as well served as Wales have by their post-war fly-halves, and even one or two before that. Four have found a place in this book and all have their claimants as the best-ever. To have to choose between Cliff Morgan, Barry John, Phil Bennett and David Watkins is a selectorial chore that would delight any panel. 'The outside-half factory' which Max Boyce sings about must really exist somewhere in Wales and the arrival of Cardiff's Gareth Davies to succeed Phil Bennett in the national side is proof that the conveyor belt is still churning out material of the highest quality.

David Watkins is a rarity in Rugby Union circles. He is a player who turned 'traitor' – that, in Welsh terms, means signing away your amateur status – yet his popular appeal and personality ensured quick forgiveness and his career up North was followed avidly in South Wales. A measure of the esteem he was held in can be judged from the fact that on his move the Welsh Rugby Union sent Watkins a letter thanking him for all he had done and wishing him well in the future. Watkins played twenty-one times for Wales before joining Salford for well over £10,000 in 1967; and twelve years later this great servant of both codes was still playing international Rugby League. It was a magnificent achievement for someone who had been playing at the highest level of Rugby for sixteen years.

Like the other Welsh fly-halves, David Watkins played an all-round game, able to adapt to the kicking or running aspect depending on the situation. His early games for Wales were played with Clive Rowlands, so kicking was very much the order of the day. In the match against Scotland at Murrayfield in 1963, the number of passes Watkins received could be counted on the fingers of one hand.

But Watkins was an exciting runner when he had the chance and one of his finest attributes was his speed off the mark, this pace taking him through defences before they had time to react. And if a match was in deadlock, there was none better than Watkins for popping up with a dropped goal to swing the game his side's way; this particular skill continued to serve him well on the Rugby League fields.

It was another sport that was his first love in his early days. Born in 1942, young Watkins was a soccer fanatic; but he was persuaded to move his loyalties, and started off as scrum-half at the Glan-yr-Afon Secondary Modern School. By the time he left there and joined the Cwmcelyn Youth

Side at the age of fifteen, Watkins was established in his outside-half berth. After two seasons in the Welsh Schools side, he joined the club with which his name will always be associated during his Union days – Newport. His progress was swift; in his first season, there were two Welsh trials and an appearance for the Barbarians; also it looked as if he should have gone out as a replacement towards the end of the 1962 Lions' tour of South Africa. With the current Welsh fly-half, Alun Rees, turning professional during the close season, Watkins had high hopes of making the national team during the following winter.

It all went according to plan and Watkins lined up as fly-half for the international against England at Cardiff in January 1963. He was not alone in making his debut that day; his scrum-half was captaining Wales on his first appearance, as he was to do in his fourteen consecutive caps. That scrum-half was Pontypool's Clive Rowlands, and David Watkins was his half-back partner in all those games. Other notable Welsh first-cap winners that day were Denzil Williams and Brian Thomas. But that afternoon Wales suffered their last defeat at the hands of England in Cardiff for the next eighteen years at least. Watkins' involvement in the next game, at Murrayfield, was one of the least active any international has spent at fly-half, but Rowlands' kicking laid the groundwork for a 6-0 Welsh win. Although the next two matches that season were lost, Watkins dropped a goal against Ireland for his first points for his country and generally gave the impression that Wales had found another quality fly-half.

The next season was even more memorable for him and he took part in a game he described by saying: 'It will always remain for me one of my treasured memories.' It was only a club game for Newport, but as the opposition were the All Blacks you can appreciate Watkins' words. A John Uzzell dropped goal seventeen minutes into the first half was enough to inflict the only defeat on Wilson Whineray's New Zealanders. All Black fly-half Earle Kirton was given a lot of the blame for the defeat, but those critics should have appreciated more the magnificent performance of that Newport side, especially the forwards and half-backs. It is a victory that will remain one of the club's finest achievements.

Watkins did not have the same luck when playing for his country against the same All Blacks, but the season generally showed an improvement for Wales. Scotland, with whom Wales shared the championship, and Ireland were both beaten, with Watkins particularly brilliant against Ireland and scoring his first try for Wales.

Part of his summer was spent with Wales in South Africa, where the visitors were badly defeated, 24-3, in the international. It was on this trip that many Welshmen realised the gulf in coaching and forward technique between the Rugby powers. The 1965 international season was Watkins' last as Clive Rowlands' partner. The Pontypool scrum-half retired after achieving one of his

David Watkins kicks for touch in his final appearance at Twickenham, the 1966 game between Wales and England which the visitors won 11-6.

ambitions – Wales's first Triple Crown since 1952. And for Watkins personally, it was another successful year; he dropped a goal against England and then scored a try against Ireland in the game that gave his country that long-awaited Triple Crown. Although a French defeat stopped them going for the Grand Slam, the championship was theirs, as it was the following year, this time with Alun Pask as captain. Watkins, in addition to his footballing skills, was now able to use his experience to control and dominate games from fly-half.

Such was the atmosphere of international Rugby at that time that he was unable to run with the ball as much as he would have liked; yet, he made the best of his opportunities and was first-choice for the Lions in their six Tests on their tour of Australasia in 1966. It was not a particularly happy tour in terms of results, but Watkins performed well considering the All Blacks' pack had the run of the field. Watkins skippered the Lions in two Tests in New Zealand, but the series was lost, four internationals to nil.

Still, the fly-half was at the top of his trade. As well as those six Lions' Tests, he had played eighteen consecutive times for Wales and seemed well in control. With the Australians touring towards the end of 1966, the Welsh selectors suggested that it might be wise for him to take a rest before the Wallaby international, especially after his arduous summer. This he did, but when the Welsh team was announced, there was a new name at fly-half . . . Barry John. It was a blow to Watkins and his pride. After seeming as secure as anyone in international Rugby, he had been dropped at the age of twenty-four. He recovered his place two games later and was also given the captaincy. Only a last-ditch ankle tap from Ken Goodall, Ireland's No. 8, stopped the skipper saving his side from a 3-0 defeat. His scrum-half in this game was Allan Lewis, but Watkins lined up with a promising newcomer for the game in Paris . . . Gareth Edwards. And in David Watkins' twenty-

first and final international, against England, another youngster marked his debut with an astonishing display. His name was Keith Jarrett, and he scored nineteen points in Wales's 34-21 victory.

Yet, although Watkins was back in the national side, his earlier dropping that season had made him think; he knew that he was only as good as his last performance and had to rely on the whims and fancies of the Welsh selectors. So when Salford made him an offer he could not refuse, he went 'North' at the age of 25. His tremendous service to both codes quashes any murmurs of cashing in; David Watkins has been a magnificent servant of both games. And while Wales missed his tactical expertise and speed off the mark – he was one of the quickest men in this respect in the past forty years – Barry John was already on the scene, as was Phil Bennett when Barry John departed, as was Gareth Davies when Phil Bennett departed. This seam of Welsh half-back gold is a long way from running out.

Wilson Whineray

Until Graham Mourie emerged on the Rugby scene in 1977, Wilson Whineray was the most popular and successful captain the All Blacks have produced since the last war. His record of twenty-two wins in thirty internationals in charge is exceptional; very few captains reach double figures skippering an international side. Although it is undeniable that he led one of the finest sets of forwards ever to grace a Rugby field, his talents as a leader ensured his players were not subject to complacency and that their enormous potential was fulfilled. Whineray took over the captaincy in only his third game – a feat emulated by Graham Mourie twenty-one years later – for the series against Australia in 1958 and was at the head of most

161

All Black triumphs until his retirement after the 1965 Test series against the Springboks.

Wilson Whineray grew in stature as his years in office increased. In only his second game in charge, the All Blacks were beaten by the Wallabies; Whineray took the defeat badly and personally. Yet that setback had its advantages; by the time England visited New Zealand in 1963 and Whineray was asked about the possibility of a home defeat, he replied philosophically: 'The world will still go on, the sun will still shine, if we get beaten.' Self-castigation after the event would not change what had passed. Whineray learnt his lessons well!

Not that Wilson James Whineray was ever ready to concede defeat; his captaincy in the third Test in South Africa in 1960 proved that. The sides had scored one victory each, so this third game was of the utmost importance. And the game looked like going the Springboks' way as they led 11-3 with six minutes to go. But a huge penalty goal from Don Clarke and his pressure conversion from the corner of a McMullen try kept the series alive for the All Blacks. The hero of the day was Clarke, but it had been Whineray who had inspired his players into believing that all was not lost and the game could still be saved.

This 'never-say-die' attitude is characteristic of the New Zealand temperament, especially for someone whose mother came from Yorkshire. Whineray himself was born in Auckland and by the time he was attending Auckland grammar school, the boy who was to become the most-capped All Black prop of all time was in the scrum-half berth. It was only in his second year there that Whineray moved to the front of the scrum.

After some provincial appearances for Wairarapa, he toured Ceylon with the NZ Colts in 1955; a fellow tourist was Colin Meads. In the following year, Whineray took part in two historic victories against the visiting 1956 Springboks, playing for Canterbury, the province he had switched to, and for NZ Universities.

Wilson Whineray races away to score that memorable final try in the All Blacks 36-3 victory over the Barbarians at Cardiff in 1964.

The national selectors had by now noted his promise and he made his debut against the Wallabies in 1957. Perhaps more importantly that year, he captained the NZ Under-23 side on their tour to Japan and his successes on and off the field marked his card as a future All Black skipper. And sure enough, he was given the job in 1958 for the three-Test series against Australia. Whineray could not have asked for a better start. Within twenty-three minutes of his captaincy he had scored two tries – his first for his country. Little did he know that these were going to be the only tries he would obtain for New Zealand; his name did not appear on the score-sheet in his next 29 appearances.

Defeat followed in the next Test and it was obvious that Whineray's personal performance was suffering from the responsibility of being in charge. Although the series was won, as was the battle with the Lions in 1959, Wilson Whineray's leadership was proving of far greater value to his country than his ability as prop. His conflict was such that he decided not to accept the captaincy for the 1960 tour to South Africa, but would concentrate on winning his place in the front row on merit.

Whineray eventually reconsidered his decision and the tour, despite the Test series being lost, was a great personal triumph for the All Blacks' captain, heralding the turning point in his career. The 1956 New Zealand–South Africa Tests had left a lot of ill-feeling between the two countries, but Whineray's side four years later went a long

way to repairing that damage. Whineray was as gracious in defeat as he was modest in victory. And, although given a hard time by du Toit, his opposing Test prop, Whineray was an important member of the team in his own right and returned to New Zealand firmly established as captain. It was the only series that Whineray ever lost as captain of the All Blacks. France, Australia and England all travelled to New Zealand with little success; so when the time came to pick the players to tour Great Britain and France in 1963-64, there was only one choice to lead them, Wilson Whineray.

Whineray and his men had an outstanding tour with only a draw at Murrayfield denying them victories over all five countries. The All Blacks were popular visitors and they reserved some of their finest Rugby for the final game of the tour – against the

163

Barbarians at Cardiff. The visitors soon found themselves three points down; points that had come from one of their own team-mates, Ian Clarke, who was guesting for the Baa-Baas that day. He drop-kicked what was later described as 'an own goal.' But that lead did not last long and the All Blacks found their form, entering the final minutes with a 31-3 lead. They launched one final attack and fed Whineray who headed for the line with colleagues inside and outside him. But the full-back went for the interception and Whineray threw the perfect dummy to score near the post. It was the final All Black try on the tour in thirty-four matches, and, perhaps, more fittingly, Whineray's first of the tour. His players congratulated him as he walked back to the half-way line, the Cardiff crowd started singing 'For He's a Jolly Good Fellow'—it was an emotional and unique experience for the New Zealand captain and all those at Cardiff that day.

Wilson Whineray was not leading the All Blacks the following season against the Wallabies, because he had decided to restrict himself to club Rugby for a season; he left his options open for returning against the Springboks the following year if he wanted to. He did, and so did the New Zealand selectors, and the fair-haired, six-foot prop returned for his finale on the international front. Also Whineray had a score to settle as the Springboks were the only blemish on his fine record as captain; he set the record straight with a 3-1 win in the series. Before that final Test, he announced that this would be his last appearance in an international and his side responded, as they had always done, with a 20-3 victory.

A measure of his achievements as captain is that the next in the list of All Black skippers when he retired was Cliff Porter who led the side seven times! Under Whineray's leadership, twenty-two of the thirty games were won, with three drawn and five lost. Between August 27, 1960 when they lost the fourth Test at Port Elizabeth to

Wilson Whineray was captain of the All Blacks in 30 of his 32 international appearances, a record for any country.

the Springboks and the third Test defeat against the same side on September 4, 1965, New Zealand were undefeated in international Rugby, winning 15 of the 17 matches. That is an amazing record and the captain must take a lot of the credit.

Whineray once said that one of the first essentials of captaincy was to obtain the confidence of your team. This he achieved to a remarkable level, because of his intelligence and his gift for reading the character of the men under his charge. Not only obtaining their confidence, but their respect and admiration. He always wanted to do the best for his team, his country and, most of all, for Rugby.

He subdued the adventurous aspect of his Rugby character, because he felt it was not in the best interests of the team and even admitted that he would never have dummied Stuart Wilson in that Barbarian's game if the All Blacks had not been that far in front.

He added: 'A captain must not take part in intrigue, and you must avoid becoming too closely acquainted with players to prevent your own feelings running away with your judgement.' This attitude may account for the thoughts of some of the younger players on the 1963-64 tour that they were being neglected by their captain. Whineray was generally upset when players were dropped, but felt that they should be able to work off their disappointment without him around; hence the feelings about being ignored which the inexperienced members of the party felt. But no-one could ever doubt his motives, commitment and dedication, and he commanded a tremendous loyalty. And rightly so; his record as captain is unsurpassed in Rugby history.

Bleddyn Williams

'The Prince of Welsh Centres', Bleddyn Williams' game revolved around perfect timing and a razor-sharp sidestep which was devastating in its effect and consequence. His career spanned a 'golden era' for Cardiff and Wales and he led both with considerable success, being paired in the centre with Jack Matthews, whose hard-tackling was legendary, and they played together many times for Wales.

Bleddyn Williams came from a very famous Rugby family; in all, there were eight boys and four girls and, amazingly, all eight brothers turned out for the Cardiff club at one time or another. Gwyn, the eldest, was one of Bleddyn's main inspirations and a top-class flanker before going to Rugby League; the last of the eight, Tony, made his debut during the 1960-61 season.

Bleddyn Williams' thirteen stone was packed into a five-foot-ten frame, yet he was a balanced runner who brought a great deal of poise and style to the midfield. An excellent passer of the ball, he knew just when to deliver the ball and wings enjoyed his company inside them. His whole game was performed with an ease which always suggested something special, and there was an unhurriedness about his play which displayed his class. Some of his early days had been spent at fly-half, but, despite an occasional hankering for his old position, he never showed the same comfort in a fly-half's boots. His deadly sidestep was one weapon which worried opposing defences; he would scythe his way through and, if there was a half-hearted tackle, his bulk travelling at speed would take him past. This sidestep was introduced early into his repertoire and practised on, and it served him well through a distinguished career.

Born in 1923, Bleddyn Williams attended the junior school in Taffs Well, as did all his brothers before and after him. Scrum-half was the position he started off in, but, by the time he was studying at Rydal, he had moved out to fly-half. Although a broken ankle kept him out of contention for a Welsh Secondary Schools place, he still played for Cardiff during his school days in the last season before the war.

Williams joined the RAF on leaving Rydal and was one of the top players in the RAF and Welsh Services sides. When the war finished, his Rugby career really took off, playing in the Victory internationals and captaining Wales against the Kiwis. Caps were not awarded for these games and Williams had to wait until the 1947 match against England before winning his Welsh cap. He played at fly-half, but looked uncomfortable and Wales never tried that experiment again. Other newcomers that day included Rees Stephens, Jack Matthews, Billy Cleaver and Ken Jones; unfortunately England somewhat spoiled the occasion by winning 9-6. Still, it was Wales's only defeat that season; Williams ran in a beautiful try against Scotland and his side shared the championship.

Cardiff had some brilliant backs at this time – Haydn Tanner, Billy Cleaver, Jack Matthews and Les Williams as well as Bleddyn Williams – and 1949-50 saw them in sparkling form. In the final game, Bleddyn Williams scored the three tries necessary to give him a tally for the season of forty-one, a new club record which still stands. Williams played in Cardiff's, Wales' and the Barbarians' victories over the visiting Australians; indeed, that club's win over the Wallabies heralded a run of twenty-two successive victories and the Barbarians' game set a precedent for the tradition that a touring side always finish their visit with a game against the Baa-Baas.

Williams was appointed captain of Cardiff in 1950 and seemed also likely to lead Wales when he was asked to skipper the Probable side in the Welsh trial. But he injured his knee, came back too soon, and did not play for Wales that season. That injury almost cost him a place on the 1950 Lions' tour of New Zealand, but he recovered and was given the vice-captaincy. His presence was invaluable and the Cardiff centre had no peer that summer. Although he missed the first Test through injury, he recovered for the rest of the international series, leading the Lions in the last two Tests, which were narrowly lost 6-3 and 11-8. The British back play had delighted New Zealand supporters throughout the tour and Bleddyn Williams was rightly recognised as one of the finest centres to have visited there.

Instead of taking a rest, Williams returned almost immediately to playing for Cardiff, but after three years of almost continuous top-class Rugby, the sparkle was missing and he was beginning to look stale. And, for the second successive season, there was no Williams in the Welsh centre. But the arrival of another touring team in Basil Kenyon's 1951-52 Springboks provided the incentive he needed, responding in fine style. In the club game against the tourists,

Williams rounded off a magnificent effort to dive over van Schoor for a try which seemed to set Cardiff on the victory-trail. With five minutes remaining, the home team were 9-8 in front, but Springbok Osche sprinted after a kick ahead to touch down and inflict one of the unluckiest defeats Cardiff have ever suffered. Later, a disappointing display by Cliff Morgan cost Wales dear in their game against South Africa. There was compensation for Welsh supporters when Williams and Malcolm Thomas worked a superb scissors for the Cardiff man to score Wales' only points in their 6-3 defeat.

Bob Stuart's All Blacks arrived in 1953-54 and this was perhaps Bleddyn Williams' and Cardiff's most memorable season. His instructions to the pack in the club game against them on November 21 were simple: 'So, it's up to you. Give me just two-fifths of the ball out there and we'll win this match. But without you we can't do it. Now, let's go.' And go they certainly did: magnificent work by the Cardiff forwards held the All Blacks' pack and tries from Judd and Rowlands saw the home side through. It was Williams who had punted ahead for Alun Thomas to pick up the ball and beat Bob Scott with the pass for Rowlands to score. What a day for Cardiff and Bleddyn Williams. He, along with the Cardiff half-backs who were now Cliff Morgan and Rex Willis, had spearheaded the plans to beat New Zealand. The centre admits: 'Those last three minutes were the longest of my life.'

I wonder how he felt when he captained Wales against the same opposition a month later. Williams had captained his country in three internationals the previous season, recording a pleasing three out of three success-rate. Could he do it again? The game would depend on whether the Welsh forwards, like Cardiff, could contain the magnificent New Zealand pack. All seemed lost when Wales were losing 8-5 with fifteen minutes to go and were without centre Gareth Griffiths who had dislocated his

Bleddyn Williams dives over Ryk van Schoor to score for Cardiff against the Springboks at Cardiff in 1951. The Springboks won 11-9 with a late try.

shoulder and with flanker Clem Thomas on the wing. But Griffiths returned to the fray when he should not have and this gesture provided the inspiration the tiring Welsh forwards needed. A penalty goal levelled the scores and then Clem Thomas hoisted that most famous and talked-about cross-kick and Ken Jones galloped away for the try which gave Wales their third, and until the end of the seventies their last, victory over New Zealand by 13-8.

Williams, who had stayed on despite suffering from torn leg ligaments in the last twenty minutes, summed it all up: 'How we came back to win, I have never understood.' Two wins over the All Blacks in a month is a fine achievement, and a rare one. Williams paid heavily; those leg ligaments kept him out of the international season until the final game.

Bleddyn Williams played his twenty-second and final game for Wales against England in 1955. He was captain again and, although the centre looked slightly sluggish in the Cardiff mud, Wales won so that Williams finished with the enviable record of victories in all his five games as Welsh captain. Subsequently the Welsh selectors dropped him; many thought it was unfair, as they did his omission from the Lions' party that was to tour South Africa that summer. Bleddyn Williams retired soon after, continuing to communicate his extensive knowledge on the game as a journalist. He had his fair share of ups and downs in an eventful career and suffered repeatedly from injuries, some from the fact that he could not resist the chance of playing, even when it might have been better to rest. Yet his contribution to Cardiff, Wales, the Barbarians and the British Lions is immeasurable; and that contribution was made with a rare ability and talent, bringing out all that is best in Rugby football.

JPR Williams

The first new-styled attacking full-back, JPR Williams was also the outstanding defender since the last war, and maybe before it. He dominated the seventies and while his attacking, try-scoring skills attracted publicity, it was his defensive play that was immaculate and his real strength. Unlike Andy Irvine, the world-class British full-back whose game revolved around his exciting running skills, JPR Williams' ventures upfield and into the line were a bonus. One would have imagined that the first prodigy of the new kicking dispensation law would have thrown caution to the wind in the new free-running adventurous atmosphere, but he never neglected his full-back duties which were defensive first and foremost.

His positional play and catching were as sure as Monday follows Sunday and Willie John McBride commented that JPR, as he was known to the Rugby world, did not drop a catch during the whole 1974 British Lions' tour of South Africa. It became a golden rule for opposing fly-halves not to kick anywhere near Williams, as it was merely giving the Welshman another opportunity to attack. Being the superb technician he was, if the seemingly impossible did happen and he did drop the ball, he would be positioned so that the ball would fall behind him. The opposition would not gain advantage from even his rare mistakes. His tackling was legendary and would normally stop the attackers as though they had walked into a brick wall— they often thought they had! His barging of French wing Gourdon into touch near the Welsh line to help win Wales a 1976 Grand Slam will live long in the crowd's memory as undoubtedly it will in Gourdon's. His stopping of opponents was never less than whole-hearted and timing and positioning were spot-on to deliver the maximum force and effect.

It is said that his line-kicking and goal-kicking were not up to the standard of Bob Scott and Don Clarke, but Williams rarely missed touch. If the kicks did not gain those few extra yards, it was not important to the forwards who just wanted the ball safely out of play. He became the first regular try-scoring full-back in international Rugby, selecting England for special treatment by scoring five of his six against them, including four at Twickenham. Williams was not an elusive runner in the style of Andy Irvine, but was powerful, strong, determined and took a lot of stopping with the line in sight. Another valuable attribute was that he would not lose possession or have the ball taken off him if caught by the opposition; this was necessary in stopping quick counter-attacks. Williams may not have been a great goal-kicker, though he was of valuable service to his country on more than one occasion, but as his career coincided with Keith Jarrett's, Barry John's, Phil Bennett's and Steve Fenwick's, it was not a department in which Wales were lacking.

All this considerable and unique talent was motivated by the fiercest competitive spirit ever seen on any sporting field. He loved the physical confrontation and was perfectly happy training with the Lions' forwards on his two tours; even he noted their improvement from 1971 to 1974.

JPR Williams was the rock on which the success of those two British Lions' tours was based. There were never any worries about their full-back missing tackles, dropping catches or letting the side down in any way. And this confidence spread through the side and gave them the motivation to beat the southern hemisphere's Rugby giants. The full-back who became the most famous sporting doctor since WG Grace was a talented games player. His skill plus strong determination helped him to win Junior Wimbledon in 1966 and he remained a top-class tennis player, despite his medical studies and Rugby career.

John Peter Rhys Williams came from a medical background. Born on March 2,

1949, both his parents were doctors in Bridgend. Educated at the local grammar school and then the famous sporting nursery, Millfield in Somerset, the youngster gained Welsh School Rugby honours as well as excelling at tennis. After playing some games for Bridgend, the medical student went to St Mary's at Paddington and joined the London Welsh club, which was blossoming under the influence of skipper John Dawes. His performance had already won him a place in the Welsh squad when he travelled with them to Argentina in 1968.

He made his international debut the following winter against Scotland at Murrayfield, along with a gangly No. 8 who went by the name of Mervyn Davies. It was a winning day for the newcomers and both were quickly recognised as players of great promise. JPR Williams was only nineteen when he was first capped for Wales and had won ten caps before he was twenty-one.

Williams was quickly establishing a reputation of being fearless and courageous, qualities he had to show in large amounts in Wales' tour of New Zealand in 1969. It was a disastrous tour with the All Blacks winning both Tests conclusively; this was the one set-back in the development of the team that was soon to dominate British Rugby. There were so many talented players available in the seventies – Gerald Davies, Dawes, John, Edwards, Mervyn Davies, Taylor and Morris as well as Williams himself and they were later joined by Bennett, Price, Fenwick, Quinnell, Windsor, Martin, and Cobner. All this vast array of Rugby skill was used to its full potential by Clive Rowlands and latterly John Dawes. Many of these players who had suffered at the hands of the All Blacks in 1969 were at the heart of the Lions' success in 1971. Williams was in superb form on that Lions' trip, earning

JPR about to get the ball away, despite the tackle, for the Barbarians in the match with the British Lions in 1977.

praise for his faultless defence and his attacking attitude. In the final Test, the full-back dropped a goal from forty-five yards, those three points helping the British side to draw the game and win the series. It was a memorable year for Williams, helping Wales to their first Grand Slam since 1952 and the Lions' first-ever win over the All Blacks in New Zealand. He was firmly established as the world's number one full-back and was still only twenty-two.

The following year saw JPR score his second successive try on visits to Twickenham, but, after winning three internationals, the trouble in Ireland prevented them playing that game. Williams was carried off in the game against Scotland with a broken jaw when he mistimed a tackle on wing Billy Steele.

He suffered another setback when Wales were beaten 19-16 by Ian Kirkpatrick's All Blacks in late 1972. JPR Williams was denied a late try for Wales when the referee adjudged that he had grounded the ball before reaching the New Zealand line. And his run of twenty-eight consecutive caps was ended when he missed the 1974 game against England at Twickenham, when injury forced his withdrawal. Wales lost that game, a rare defeat, and with it went the international championship.

All the British players combined for the 1974 Lions' tour of South Africa. Willie John McBride described his number one full-back in this way: 'Without him, I would very much doubt if the Lions would have enjoyed the degree of success they did on those two tours. I do not think he dropped even one ball in South Africa and that is its own testimony to his ability in a country that is so demanding and where more often than not the ball comes out of a very bright sky. His performances have been unsurpassed in my experience.'

Barry John, who played in many inter-

The rock of the Welsh defence in the seventies, JPR Williams, kicks ahead in the third Test between the Lions and South Africa in 1974.

nationals for Wales and the Lions with Williams said: 'His part in the golden era of Welsh Rugby needs to be underlined. He knew exactly when a move was "on" and, just as important, he knew when a move was "off". His entrances into the line and his customary decoy runs were perfect pieces of Rugby. The subtle things he got up to were not always appreciated by spectators. For such a big man he has considerable grace.'

Williams was in devastating form throughout the tour. His barging run in the final minutes of the fourth Test set up the Fergus Slattery try which was disallowed thus denying the Lions twenty-two victories in twenty-two appearances; they had to be content with a 3-0 victory in the series with that final game drawn.

The second half of the seventies saw another golden era for Wales—four championships, four Triple Crowns and two Grand Slams—all in the space of five years. One by one the old guard was dropping out— Mervyn Davies, Gareth Edwards, Phil

Bennett and Gerald Davies—leaving only JPR to carry on. By now he had qualified as a doctor and was back in Wales specialising in surgery. His work meant he had missed the 1977 Lions' tour. Playing again for Bridgend, he was elected to captain them in their centenary year, 1978-79; it was a busy season for him as he also took over the leadership of Wales. It was also an eventful time. He became the centre of the incident in which All Black prop John Ashworth ripped open the full-back's face in the club game against New Zealand.

On the playing side, although Wales lost by a single point to the All Blacks and France, they won the Triple Crown for the fourth successive season. Six weeks later, Williams led Bridgend to victory in the Schweppes/WRU Cup final over Pontypridd. It was to be his last season of international Rugby and the most famous full-back in the history of Rugby retired with fifty-two caps, one behind the Welsh record set by Gareth Edwards.

JPR hoped to remain in Rugby and help set up a sports clinic with special emphasis on injuries sustained in Rugby. In his final international appearance he was rightly acclaimed by the Welsh supporters; he had been their favourite for over a decade and his presence, confidence and determination at the back of the Welsh defence was something the Cardiff crowd would miss, but certainly not forget.

Rhys Williams

The best second-row forward produced by Britain since the last war and the outstanding forward on the Lions' tours of 1955 and 1959. Totally uncompromising in his play, he was a rarity in that he combined all the skills that most locks specialise in. The ideal pairing is said to be a good jumper with a strong, mauling, powerful player as a partner. Rhys Williams was all these things and more. A man of immense strength, Williams was a mauler of the top-bracket and was once described thus by his Welsh captain, flanker Clem Thomas: 'You never heard Rhys, but, by God, you felt his presence.'

For a man of over six foot three, weighing over sixteen-and-a-half stone, he was remarkably agile and was a key man in the line-out. Not that his worth was restricted to the set pieces and rucks and mauls, but also in the loose, where his speed around the park belied his size. And when he hit a ruck or maul, it was seen to move. With complete dedication and commitment, his approach to Rugby was impeccable; always clean and fair if allowed to be, yet he knew the need to stand up for himself or more probably his colleagues. It is true that the Lions' forwards in his two tours would have been lost without him; his presence was always an inspiration to the players

around him. And how much better the other second-row performed when he was packing down with Rhys Williams in the engine-room of the scrum.

His opponents respected him, too, and his 'no-messing' style of power Rugby earned him the highest regard in New Zealand and South Africa, so often the graveyards of British forwards.

Rhys Haydn Williams was born in Cwmllynfell, West Wales in July 1930, the son of a colliery blacksmith. It was the classic Welsh Rugby background and young Williams was in the Ystalyfera Grammar School first team at the age of fifteen. Four years later, while studying for a science honours degree at the University of Wales (which he attained), Williams made his debut for Llanelli at Stradey Park. He was still developing as a forward, but progressed quickly and was showing great promise when he played his first major game, for the

for the Test team. Cliff Morgan recalls a time when Williams, as usual, had given his all for the side. It was at the end of the 'Greatest Match' – the first Test, which the Springboks lost 22-23. Morgan remembers: 'At the end, when we were delirious with joy at having won by the odd point in forty-five, Williams collapsed from exhaustion. His enormous frame, lying like a mortal coil on the frost-brown Ellis Park, revealed the price of victory. It's a sight that will always live with me.'

He was to repeat these outstanding displays for the Lions four years later in New Zealand and, if anything, surpassed his previous standard. New Zealand Rugby supporters are shrewd judges of forward talent and they bracketed Williams with the best as he used his intelligence to utilise his many talents to the full. At the end of that 1959 series, five outstanding players from the Tests were selected as the best of the tour, and Rhys Williams was the only forward.

Rugby, at all times, was a sport to Williams and a game to be enjoyed, but to be played with no less than one hundred percent effort and commitment. All that commitment was required in the fourth and final Test at Auckland, when he repeatedly denied the All Blacks' line-out possession as the home side tried to recover from the 6-9 deficit. Williams and the Lions held out for their only victory of the series. At the end of the tour, he had played in ten consecutive Tests for the Lions, always at the corner-stone of their pack. And the respect that colleague and opponent alike paid him was something he treasured dearly. They, like him, had been through the mill and knew the qualities that Williams possessed that made him stand out in the crowd.

He returned home to play in one more international for his country and it was not the occasion he had hoped it would be. In

club against Basil Kenyon's 1950-51 Springboks. His apprenticeship continued and in 1954 Williams made his international debut for Wales; the most influential British forward of the fifties had arrived.

Williams had won six caps for his country by the time he was selected to tour South Africa with the British Lions' party in the summer of 1955. His contribution was considerable, though the second-row admits it was a talented tour party: 'Maybe, I think, that was the best tour I ever went on, because it was the first, and there's always something extra about the first time you do anything. But, let's be fair, the team had everything. Good and honest forwards with backs who wanted to run. You could depend on backs finishing for you after you had fought for possession. I liked that.'

Williams produced peak form in South Africa, a peak which lasted for the whole tour and he was always an automatic choice

his twenty-third and final game, he was given the captaincy of Wales to add to the honours in leading Llanelli and, once, the British Lions. As the game approached, he fell low to a heavy cold and tried to sweat it out; although able to take the field, Williams had taken a lot out of himself. Richard Sharp then proceeded to take a lot out of Wales on his debut and Williams' side was fourteen points down at half-time, eventually losing 14-6. Williams was dropped, along with familiar names such as Faull, Terry Davies and Hadyn Morgan. Williams, unlike the other three, was not recalled and he retired at the end of the season. Williams had played in some memorable Welsh sides, but never won the Grand Slam or Triple Crown during his reign; there was only one outright championship win in that period, too.

Williams had travelled all over the world in his playing career. There were Lions' visits to South Africa and New Zealand and tours with the Barbarians to Canada (1957) and South Africa again (1958). In 1957 he even went to Moscow as captain of Llanelli in a Rugby competition. Always a popular visitor, he was one of the game's finest ambassadors, communicating to everyone his love for Rugby. Without him, British Rugby, especially among the forwards, would have been much poorer in the fifties. Many of his colleagues looked to him to show the way and Rhys Williams never let them down.

Data Table

The table below lists information about the fifty players included in this book, to the end of the 1978–79 season

Name	Country	Clubs	Position	Length of International Career	Debut and Result	Caps
Bennett, Phil	Wales	Llanelli	Fly-half	1969–78	v France 8–8	29(8)
Brown, Gordon	Scotland	W. of Scotland	Lock	1969–76	v S. Africa 6–3	30(8)
Butterfield, Jeff	England	Northampton	Centre	1953–59	v France 11–0	28(4)
Catchpole, Ken	Australia	New South Wales	Scrum-half	1961–68	v Fiji 24–6	27
Clarke, Don	New Zealand	Waikato	Full-back	1956–64	v S. Africa 17–10	31
Cotton, Fran	England	Loughborough Colls. Coventry Sale	Prop	1971–	v Scotland 15–16	25(7)
Crauste, Michel	France	Racing Club de France	Flanker	1958–66	v Scotland 11–9	43
Dauga, Benoit	France	S Montois	Lock	1964–72	v Scotland 10–0	50
Davies, Gerald	Wales	Cardiff London Welsh Loughborough Colls. Cambridge Univ.	Wing	1966–78	v Australia 11–14	46(5)

Name	Country	Clubs	Position	Length of International Career	Debut and Result	Caps
Davies, Mervyn	Wales	London Welsh Swansea	No. 8	1969–76	v Australia 16–<u>19</u>	38(8)
Duckham, David	England	Coventry	Centre	1969–76	v Ireland 17–<u>15</u>	36(3)
Edwards, Gareth	Wales	Cardiff	Scrum-half	1967–78	v France 20–<u>14</u>	53(10)
Elliott, Douglas	Scotland	Edinburgh Academy	Flanker	1947–54	v England 24–<u>5</u>	29
Gibson, Mike	Ireland	Cambridge Univ. NIFC	Centre	1964–78	v England 5–<u>18</u>	67(12)
Going, Sid	New Zealand	North Auckland	Scrum-half	1967–77	v Australia <u>29</u>–9	29
Gray, Ken	New Zealand	Wellington	Prop	1963–69	v Ireland 5–<u>6</u>	24
Greyling, Piet	S. Africa	Orange Free State	Flanker	1967–72	v France <u>26</u>–3	25
Hopwood, Douglas	S. Africa	Western Province	No. 8	1960–65	v Scotland 18–10	22
Irvine, Andy	Scotland	Heriot's FP	Full-back	1973–	v New Zealand <u>9</u>–14	32(6)
Jackson, Peter	England	Coventry	Wing	1956–63	v Wales 3–<u>8</u>	20(5)
John, Barry	Wales	Llanelli Cardiff	Fly-half	1966–72	v Australia <u>11</u>–14	25(5)
Johnson, Peter	Australia	New South Wales	Hooker	1959–72	v British Lions 6–17	42
Kirkpatrick, Ian	New Zealand	Canterbury Poverty Bay	Flanker	1967–77	v France 15–<u>21</u>	39
Kyle, Jackie	Ireland	Queen's Univ. NIFC	Fly-half	1947–58	v England <u>22</u>–0	46(6)
Laidlaw, Chris	New Zealand	Otago Oxford Univ. Canterbury	Scrum-half	1963–70	v France 3–<u>12</u>	20
McBride, Willie John	Ireland	Ballymena	Lock	1962–75	v England 16–<u>0</u>	63(17)
McLauchlan, Ian	Scotland	Jordanhill	Prop	1969–	v England 8–<u>3</u>	42(8)
McLoughlin, Ray	Ireland	Gosforth	Prop	1962–75	v England 16–<u>0</u>	40(3)
Maso, Jo	France	RC Narbonne	Centre	1967–73	v Scotland <u>8</u>–9	17
Meads, Colin	New Zealand	King Country	Lock	1957–71	v Australia 11–<u>25</u>	55
Meredith, Bryn	Wales	St. Luke's College London Welsh Newport	Hooker	1954–62	v France <u>19</u>–13	34(8)

Name	Country	Clubs	Position	Length of International Career	Debut and Result	Caps
Mias, Lucien	France	SC Mazamet	Prop	1951–59	v England 3–11	25
Morgan, Cliff	Wales	Cardiff	Fly-half	1951–58	v France 8–3	29(4)
Mourie, Graham	New Zealand	Taranaki	Flanker	1977–	v British Lions 19–7	8
O'Reilly, Tony	Ireland	Old Belvedere Leicester	Wing	1955–70	v England 6–6	29(10)
du Preez, Frik	S. Africa	Northern Transvaal	Lock	1960–71	v England 0–5	38
Price, Graham	Wales	Pontypool	Prop	1975–	v France 10–25	24(4)
Pullin, John	England	Bristol	Hooker	1966–76	v Wales 6–11	42(7)
Rives, Jean-Pierre	France	S. Toulous-ain	Flanker	1975–	v England 20–27	21
Scotland, Ken	Scotland	Heriot's FP Cambridge Univ. Leicester	Full-back	1957–65	v England 16–3	27(5)
Scott, Bob	New Zealand	Auckland	Full-back	1946–54	v Australia 31–8	17
Sharp, Richard	England	Oxford Univ. Wasps Redruth	Fly-half	1960–67	v Wales 14–6	14(2)
du Toit, Piet	S. Africa	Western Province	Prop	1958–61	v France 3–3	14
Tremain, Kel	New Zealand	Canterbury Auckland Hawke's Bay	Flanker	1959–68	v British Lions 11–8	38
de Villiers, Dawie	S. Africa	Western Province	Scrum-half	1962–70	v British Lions 8–3	25
Watkins, David	Wales	Newport	Fly-half	1963–67	v England 6–13	21(6)
Whineray, Wilson	New Zealand	Canterbury Waikato Auckland	Prop	1957–65	v Australia 6–25	32
Williams, Bleddyn	Wales	Cardiff	Centre	1947–55	v Australia 6–0	22(5)
Williams, JPR	Wales	London Welsh	Full-back	1969–78	v Australia 16–19	52(8)
Williams, Rhys	Wales	Llanelli	Lock	1954–60	v France 19–13	23(10)

NOTES: In the result column, the underlined score is that of the player's team; the first score is that of the home team.
In the caps column, the number in parenthesis is the number of Tests played for the British Lions.